THE LINCOLN ASSASSINATION IN AMERICAN HISTORY

Other titles *in American History*

IN AMERICAN HISTORY

THE LINCOLN ASSASSINATION IN AMERICAN HISTORY

Robert Somerlott

Enslow Publishers, Inc.

44 Fadem Road   PO Box 38
Box 699   Aldershot
Springfield, NJ 07081   Hants GU12 6BP
USA   UK

Library of Congress Cataloging-in-Publication Data

Somerlott, Robert.
    The Lincoln assassination in American history / Robert Somerlott.
       p. cm. — (In American history)
    Includes bibliographical references and index.
    Summary: Discusses the people and events connected with the
assassination of Abraham Lincoln, as well as its effect on the history of the
United States.
    ISBN 0-89490-886-3
      1. Lincoln, Abraham, 1809–1865—Assassination—Juvenile literature.
2. United States—Politics and government—1861–1865—Juvenile
literature. [1. Lincoln, Abraham, 1809–1865—Assassination. 2. United
States—Politics and government—1861–1865.] I. Title. II. Series.
E457.5.S68 1998
973.7′092—dc21   97-23480
                                                   CIP
                                                    AC

Illustration Credits: Enslow Publishers, Inc., p. 72; The Lincoln
Museum, Fort Wayne, IN, pp. 10, 11, 17, 23, 28, 35, 37, 49, 57, 67, 68,
77, 85, 98, 117; National Archives, pp. 12, 19, 21, 42, 50, 60, 70, 91,
104, 107, 113.

Cover Illustrations: The Lincoln Museum, Fort Wayne, IN; National
Archives.

★ CONTENTS ★

IN FORD'S THEATRE

The audience crowding Ford's Theatre that night was in a festive mood. Ladies in hoop skirts had donned their new spring bonnets, gay with French ribbons and silk roses. The men also looked elegant in knee-length frock coats. They wore high white collars and black stovepipe hats. As always in Washington during these years, the theater was sprinkled with men in blue army uniforms. The flickering gaslights gleamed on their brass buttons. That would soon change. Military dress would become less common in the nation's capital. The terrible Civil War that had wracked the nation for four bitter years was over at last.

Day after day, the telegraph wires had hummed with good news from the victorious Union armies fighting in the South. Richmond, Virginia, capital of the rebel Confederacy, had fallen on April 3, 1865. This had caused the wildest celebration Washington had ever seen. A newspaper editor at the *Washington Star*, one of the first men to learn about Richmond, ran to a blackboard in front of the *Star* building. He printed big letters in chalk:

GLORY!!!   HAIL COLUMBIA!!!
HALLELUJAH!!!   RICHMOND OURS!!![1]

Soon, cannons roared and bugles blared. People surged through the streets shouting and cheering.

The city was still rejoicing six days later when the best news of all came. General Robert E. Lee had surrendered his Southern army at a small town called Appomattox Court House. Could the war really be over?

Any lingering doubt about the Union victory had ended two days earlier. Bells rang and bands played to celebrate the capture of Montgomery, Alabama, the city that had been the first capital of the Confederacy. The long struggle that had cost Americans so much suffering had truly ended. President Abraham Lincoln, who had guided the United States to victory, was hailed as the nation's hero and savior.

A Celebration in a Theater

It was known that President Lincoln would be attending Ford's Theatre on the evening of April 14, 1865. James R. Ford, brother of the owner, John, and business manager of the playhouse, had advertised this to the whole city in handbills that read:

THIS EVENING
The Performance Will Be Honored
By The Presence Of
PRESIDENT LINCOLN[2]

Lincoln was a major attraction amid the celebrations. In fact, his announced attendance was the reason why this Good Friday performance of the comedy *Our American Cousin* had almost sold out. Although the play was not a new one, 1,675 people had bought seats for the performance that night. John Ford's advertising had worked. Many of the ticket holders would not have paid to watch this familiar comedy. They simply wanted to see President Lincoln.

One such person was James Ferguson, owner of a restaurant next door to the theater. He had bought seats at the end of a row where he could have a good view of the presidential box, which Lincoln was expected to occupy. Ferguson had brought with him a little girl, the daughter of a neighbor, because they both wanted to see the famous Abraham Lincoln.

Now at 8:00 P.M. when the curtain was about to rise, they were disappointed. The presidential box, up a short flight of stairs, was at one side of the building. It was not above the auditorium, but over the front part of the stage. Its opening had been so heavily decorated with flags and patriotic streamers that Ferguson's view was almost blocked. It appeared that the box was empty. Could President Lincoln have changed his mind? Was he not coming after all? So it seemed when the orchestra leader, Professor Withers, lifted his baton and the musicians began the overture. Moments later, the curtains opened and *Our American Cousin* began.

The first act was well under way when there was a stir in the house. The action on stage halted. Abraham

This is Ford's Theatre, with five arched doorways, as it appeared in 1865. At the time, it was said to be the best playhouse in America, with the newest gas lighting and finest scenery. Today, it is both a theater and a museum.

Lincoln, delayed by business at the White House, had arrived late.

Actress Laura Keene, star of the play, moved to the footlights and clapped her hands. Then the whole audience rose, applauding. President and Mrs. Lincoln, along with a young man and woman who were their guests, entered. They went up the stairs, then moved behind the dress-circle seats toward the presidential box. (The dress circle is a section in a theater specially reserved for people wearing formal clothing.)

The orchestra played "Hail to the Chief," the music used to announce presidents. Then the gaslights were lowered again, and the play resumed.

Over the next two hours, as *Our American Cousin* continued, James Ferguson and his young companion kept glancing toward the presidential box. They hoped to catch at least a glimpse of the great man, but they were unsuccessful. Then, a few minutes after 10:00, Ferguson nudged the little girl. Lincoln was leaning forward, looking down at the audience. His left hand rested on the low wall that served as a railing for the box.

The little girl nodded and gazed at the kindly but hollow-cheeked face of the president. His was a face worn by care and responsibility. Lincoln's features were anything but handsome. In fact, people had often described him as ugly, even ape-like. Yet many who met him were struck by

Two months before his assassination, President Abraham Lincoln posed for this photograph to help an artist who was painting the president's portrait. Few pictures have shown Lincoln's gentle strength so clearly.

the strength, gentleness, and sometimes the sadness of his expression. He had such character that no one would ever forget him.

So the little girl saw Abraham Lincoln for the first—and also the last—time.

Only a few minutes later, a pistol was fired in the dimness of the presidential box. The sound was so muffled that only a few people heard it. James Ferguson, astonished, looked up to see a shadowy,

The assassin, brandishing a knife, ran across the stage. An artist recreated the scene from the testimony of the many witnesses who watched in shock and surprise.

dark-haired man climb over the ledge of the box, cling there a second, then drop to the stage. It was a long fall, eleven feet from the ledge to the floor.

A piercing scream sounded from the presidential box. Many thought the cry was uttered by Mrs. Lincoln. The dark-haired man said something most people could not hear. Then he hobbled swiftly across the stage and vanished. Alarmed spectators saw he was brandishing a long knife, which appeared to be bloody.

Within seconds, Ford's Theatre was in an uproar. The audience did not know what had happened but sensed that something terrible and unexpected had taken place.

Actress Laura Keene was one of the first to realize the truth. She stepped to the footlights of the stage to shout the news that would soon shock the entire nation.

"The president is shot! The president is shot!"[3]

2

A PRESIDENT IN DANGER

From the day of his election, the threat of being murdered hung over Abraham Lincoln. This was a danger that no other United States president had ever faced, even though American politics had always been full of name-calling and insults.

The first president George Washington had been accused of wanting to be king. President Andrew Jackson and his wife were savagely denounced in the press, and Jackson was once physically assaulted. Even mild-mannered James Buchanan, Lincoln's predecessor in the White House, was brutally treated by editors on both sides of the slavery question. Yet no one ever went so far as to demand that blood be shed.

So despite hot-tempered political disagreements, no president had ever been assassinated. Such a crime was thought to be "foreign to America."[1] Secretary of State William Henry Seward, best remembered today for the American purchase of Alaska, once said, "Assassination is not an American practice or habit." He felt that an act "so vicious and so desperate" simply could not take place in this country.[2]

Many people were slow to realize that America had become a different place by the year 1860, but Abraham Lincoln was one of the first to discover this change. It was said that in a drawer of his desk he kept a folder holding more than eighty hate-filled letters, all of them threatening him with a violent death.[3]

Most of these letters were written by Southerners enraged by Lincoln's opposition to slavery—men who feared the loss of laborers they considered their property, and thus, destruction of their way of life. Other threats came from men in the North who sympathized with the South and felt that Lincoln's policies would surely destroy the union of states.

Lincoln was elected to the presidency by the electoral college. Because the country was so deeply divided, he won only 40 percent of the popular vote. He carried every Northern and Pacific Coast state but no others. In the South, Lincoln's name was not even printed on the ballots.

Lincoln's Debates with Douglas

Stephen Douglas, long a political rival of Abraham Lincoln, won the second-most votes. It had been public debates between Lincoln and Douglas that had first brought Lincoln to national prominence in 1858. Lincoln and Douglas ran against each other for an Illinois seat in the United States Senate. Views expressed in these impassioned arguments showed not only the deep differences in the candidates but the disagreements splitting the nation.

The debates, held in several Illinois towns, featured brass bands and fireworks. Red, white, and blue banners decorated the fronts of buildings. Thousands flocked from the countryside to hear the fierce exchange of views and see a spectacle the whole nation was following in newspapers.

The two men were as different in physical appearance as in their political stances. Lincoln stood six feet four inches tall, and he looked like a son of the prairies. Gaunt and wiry, he was a pioneer who had split logs for rails, poled boats down rivers, and harvested corn. Although awkward and gangling, as a youth he had been an athlete, the one who could run the fastest, leap the widest creek, jump the highest over a fence.

Douglas presented himself as a man of the cities. He dressed elegantly in ruffled shirts and wide-brimmed felt hats. Only five feet four inches tall, he was nicknamed the "Little Giant" because of his powerful voice and commanding presence. Douglas looked dapper and smooth, a complete contrast to the rumpled, sometimes dusty Abraham Lincoln, who appeared to "unwind himself" before he started to speak.[4]

The public image the two candidates presented was not entirely true. Lincoln was much more than a backwoods rail-splitter, while Douglas was not as sophisticated and "citified" as he looked.

Douglas urged that slavery continue in any state or territory where the majority of the people wanted it. He seemed indifferent to the right or wrong of

Stephen Douglas, the "Little Giant," debated Lincoln seven times in 1858. Douglas wanted each state to decide about slavery for itself. His refusal to take sides won him a seat in the Senate, but later helped him lose the presidency.

the issue. But Douglas envisioned no end to forced servitude and expressed horror at the idea of freedom for African Americans.

"I am opposed to racial equality," Douglas said. "I believe this government was made by white men to be administered by the white man."[5]

Lincoln disagreed sharply. Speaking to a crowd of more than twelve thousand people and to millions more through reports telegraphed to newspapers, he said, "There is no reason in the world why the Negro is not entitled to all natural rights enumerated in the Declaration of Independence, the right to life, liberty, and the pursuit of happiness. I hold that he is as much entitled to these as the white man."[6]

Those were fighting words, opinions that would arouse the unending hatred of slave owners and their supporters. Also, such views were politically risky in Illinois, where racial prejudice ran deep. Although slavery was banned in the state, African Americans were denied such civil rights as voting, schooling, and election to public office.

Sometimes during the debates, Douglas twisted the arguments. Lincoln claimed he hid the truth by "a fantastic arrangement of words, by which a man can prove a horse chestnut to be a chestnut horse."[7] The real argument was about slavery. Would it be allowed to grow or slowly die?

Even though Lincoln's Republican party won more popular votes than the Democratic party, Lincoln lost his race for the Senate because the Democrats won the

RAN AWAY!

FROM THE SUBSCRIBER. My Mulatto Boy, GEORGE. Said George is 5 feet 8 inches in height, brown curly Hair, dark coat. I will give $400 for him alive, and the same sum for satisfactory proof that he has been killed.

Vide ANTHONY & ELLIS' MAMMOTH "UNCLE TOM'S CABIN." WM. HARRIS.

Owners of slaves who ran away printed posters like this one. Often, the same reward was offered "dead or alive." The matter of fugitive slaves bitterly divided the country at the time of the Lincoln-Douglas debates.

majority of seats in the Illinois state legislature, and they made the final decision. Only two years later, however, Lincoln won the election for the United States presidency, defeating his old foe Stephen Douglas and two other proslavery candidates.

Early Danger Signals

During the campaign, Douglas warned the country about the peril of electing Lincoln. War would result, he said: "A war of the North against the South, of the free states against the slave states—a war of extermination."[8]

It quickly appeared that Douglas's dark prediction would come true. The country was like a tightly covered tea kettle that had been simmering over a low fire. Time after time, it had hissed and bubbled, threatening to explode. The election of Lincoln threw new fuel on the fire, and the kettle had to erupt. A newspaper in Atlanta, *Confederacy*, proclaimed defiantly that "The South will never submit to such humiliation and degradation as the inauguration of Abraham Lincoln."[9] It went on to foretell mangled bodies heaped high in front of the White House and a river of blood flowing in the nation's capital. Another newspaper, *The Banner*, in Raleigh, North Carolina, spoke of "the horrors of civil war."[10]

In the midst of such a storm of fear and anger, the number of threatening letters being sent to Lincoln began to grow. The first letters were sent to Lincoln's home in Springfield, Illinois, weeks before the newly elected president left for Washington.

The letter writers blamed Lincoln for endangering the country. He had long been called "Ape Lincoln" by his opponents. Now the ape became "a baboon," "a monster," "an idiot." Some letters expressed hope he would soon be "hanged" or "burned," while others prayed for his flogging or death by torture. A mysterious group calling itself "oath-bound brotherhoods" sent pen drawings of daggers and gallows.[11] Never had a president been greeted with such menacing outcries, such fury.

A few writers who had heard about the threats sent suggestions for Lincoln's safety. One woman urged Lincoln to guard against poisoning by hiring a taster to sample all his food. Lincoln did not follow the advice and the job of presidential taster was never created.

A metal worker in Iowa explained how he would make Lincoln a

Lincoln, the newly elected president, is hoisted on Southern bayonets. Hostile cartoons appeared in many newspapers after Lincoln's election. This cartoonist had not yet learned that Lincoln had grown a beard.

shirt of flexible chain armor. He proposed plating this bulletproof garment with gold so "perspiration shall not affect it." In other words, Lincoln would not need to worry about rusting his own armor by sweating. "It could be covered with silk and worn over an ordinary undershirt."[12]

Another suggestion for saving Lincoln's life was a proposal that he resign his office at the inaugural ceremony and name Stephen Douglas as president in his place.

Lincoln ignored both the threats and the well-meant ideas to protect him. But later he said, "I believe there are men who want to take my life. If anyone is willing to give his life for mine, there is nothing can prevent it."[13]

Mrs. Lincoln Is Frightened

Lincoln's wife, Mary Todd Lincoln, was far less calm and accepting of danger. Born to an aristocratic Kentucky family and considered a Southern belle in her youth, Mary was an intelligent but high-strung woman of nervous disposition. She suffered from migraine headaches, with attacks so severe that she was often left almost helpless for days on end. Such suffering no doubt added to her nervousness and quick temper. Later, Lincoln's young male secretaries in the White House nicknamed Mrs. Lincoln the "hell cat" and tried hard to stay out of her way.[14]

At the same time, Mary Todd Lincoln was impulsively kind and generous, as well as a devoted mother.

Mary Todd Lincoln was frightened by the death threats her husband received even before the Lincolns reached Washington, D.C. Her frail nerves and quick temper caused her much unhappiness.

She tried hard to make her husband's life easier and more pleasant, a task sometimes too much for her frail temperament.

Shortly before the Lincoln family left Springfield for Washington, something happened that caused Mrs. Lincoln great fear and distress, setting her nerves on edge before she even reached the White House.

In those days just after the election, Mary Todd Lincoln felt unusually joyful and excited about the future. She pictured herself as First Lady, a position she had longed for but hardly dared to dream of reaching. As she went about her home supervising the packing, she was already planning her costume for the inaugural ball, a stylish blue dress with a necklace and bracelets of gold and pearls.[15]

In this happy mood, Mrs. Lincoln entered a room where a large package addressed to her husband had just arrived and was being unwrapped. She paused, thinking perhaps it was a gift some admirer had sent, then stood trembling with fright when she saw what the package contained.

It was a picture, painted with oil on canvas, showing Abraham Lincoln painfully covered with hot tar and feathers. His big hands were chained, and a hangman's rope had been knotted around his neck.[16]

Mrs. Lincoln gasped and drew back. She would remember her panic for years afterward. The ugly picture seemed to her a terrible omen, a sign of what lay ahead for her and her family in Washington, D.C.

Lincoln left Springfield in February 1861 to go by train to Washington, D.C., where he would be inaugurated as president of the United States.

It was a stormy day. Sheets of rain beat down on the roof of his carriage. Through the rain-streaked windows, he could see that the people of the town were crowding the streets to wave good-bye to him.

A PLOT IS UNCOVERED

At the railroad station, soldiers lined the way to the train. Friends packed the waiting room to shake hands with Lincoln and wish him well.

Lincoln had not expected to speak that day. Yet he was so moved by the sight of his friends that he stepped onto the rear platform of the last car of the train. He said:

> My friends, no one not in my situation can appreciate my feelings of sadness at this parting. To this place, to the kindness of these people, I owe everything. Here I have lived a quarter of a century, and have passed from a young man to an old man. Here my children have been born, and one is buried. I now leave, not knowing when or whether ever I may return.[1]

He went on to speak of the hard tasks that lay ahead of him and asked for their prayers. It was a short speech but a beautiful one, spoken as rain fell hard upon him, streaming down his lined cheeks.

Then the whistle blew, the engine started, and Lincoln was carried away. The people of Springfield stood waving good-bye in the rain. They waited silently until the train had disappeared, as though they felt they would never see their friend again.

A Perilous Journey

As the train moved through the cold rain, another kind of storm was sweeping the country, one of anger and protest. Throughout the South, meetings of furious citizens were called. Excited speakers shouted that they would give up their lives before giving up their slaves.

On the day Lincoln began his journey, Burton Craige from North Carolina rose in the House of Representatives to propose a law that would force Lincoln to recognize the independence of the Confederate states.

Violent speeches for both sides were delivered across the land. Southern politicians called on Governor Beriah Magoffin of Kentucky, trying to persuade him to lead his state in withdrawing from the Union. Lincoln's election, they claimed, "was a decree of racial equality, a signal to the Southern Negroes to kill their masters, burn the barns and crops."[2]

There was no evidence that such things were about to happen, but frightened people were ready to believe the worst.

On the train, Lincoln was guarded by friends. One of his protectors was Ward Hill Lamon. Lamon was broad shouldered and powerful, with wavy brown hair and a bushy beard. He was the United States marshal for the District of Columbia. Lincoln knew he could count on his friend Lamon. They were so close that "they could quarrel and still be friends."[3]

Lamon was worried about Lincoln's safety on the train trip. With the many stops that were planned, it would take eleven days to go from Springfield to Washington, D.C. Lincoln intended to stop in several cities and a number of smaller towns. He would meet with important officials, deliver more than twenty speeches, and shake hands with thousands of people.

It was the handshaking and the mixing with huge crowds that alarmed Lamon. He could see no way of protecting his friend Lincoln and no way of persuading him to be careful. So Lamon took his own precautions. In a suitcase, he packed several knives, pistols, brass knuckles, and a blackjack.

A Nation Dividing

Meanwhile, all over the country, new threats were being made against the president-elect.

In Indianapolis, Indiana, Lincoln spoke to a cheering crowd of twenty thousand people, urging them to "rise up and preserve the Union and liberty."[4]

Several of Lincoln's friends left the train at Indianapolis to return to Springfield. One of them said to Lamon, who was going on to Washington, "We

Big and broad shouldered, Ward Hill Lamon was a tough United States marshal. He appointed himself bodyguard for his friend Abraham Lincoln and traveled to Washington, D.C., heavily armed with guns and knives.

entrust the sacred life of Mr. Lincoln to your hands. And if you don't protect it, never return to Illinois for we will murder you on sight."[5]

It was a joke, of course, but it showed how much the danger of assassination was on everyone's mind.

On Lincoln's fifty-second birthday, he was crossing eastern Indiana and moving into Ohio. In Cincinnati, Ohio, a huge, cheering crowd greeted Lincoln. Hundreds of flags flapped in the cold February wind, and brass bands played stirring music.

During the celebration in Cincinnati, no one forgot that Kentucky, a slave state, lay just across the Ohio River. Kentucky was bitterly divided over whether or not to preserve the Union. Lamon worried that hotheads from Kentucky might slip across the river and attack Lincoln. Fortunately, it did not happen.

That same day, February 13, 1861, in Washington, Congress officially named Abraham Lincoln the president of the United States. The Capitol Building was manned with extra guards for fear that a riot might erupt. Treasury Secretary John A. Dix sent a telegram to New Orleans, Louisiana, saying, "If anyone attempts to haul down the American flag, shoot him on the spot."[6]

Lincoln's train rolled north to Columbus, Ohio, where Lincoln addressed the state legislature. Again, there were cheers and wild applause. As the presidential party continued on to Pittsburgh, Pennsylvania, and New York state, Lincoln's friends grew less worried. Whatever happened elsewhere, people in these Northern cities supported Lincoln.

In Westfield, New York, Lincoln spoke briefly from the rear of the train, then announced that someone from the town had written him, and that he would like to meet her.

"Who is she?" the crowd shouted.

"Grace Bedell," said Lincoln.

Grace, a little girl, was brought to the platform, and Lincoln said, "She wrote me that I would be better looking if I wore whiskers. You see, I have let these whiskers grow for you, Grace."[7] Then he kissed her.

Allan Pinkerton, Detective

All went well for Lincoln in the next few cities. Then in Philadelphia, Pennsylvania, Lincoln was shaking hands with people when one of his secretaries, John Nicolay, pushed through the crowd and said, "Mr. Lincoln, I must see you at once. It is an emergency."[8]

Lincoln was led to a hotel room and introduced to Allan Pinkerton, one of the first official detectives in the United States. Pinkerton had formed America's first detective agency. One of its jobs had been smuggling slaves to freedom along the route from the South to the North called the Underground Railroad.

Allan Pinkerton said, "We have come to know, Mr. Lincoln, that there exists a plot to assassinate you. The attempt will be made on your way through Baltimore, day after tomorrow. I am here to help in outwitting the assassins."

Lincoln's smile faded. He said, "I am listening, Mr. Pinkerton."[9]

Pinkerton had been working undercover in Baltimore, Maryland, posing as a man from Georgia who favored slavery. He had learned the details of the plot. Even the chief of police of Baltimore seemed to be a party to the murder plan, or at least he would not prevent it.

In Baltimore, it would be necessary for Lincoln to travel by horse-drawn carriage through part of the city from one train station to another. That was when the assassins would strike. The police chief would send only a small force to protect the president. Then a gang of thugs would start a riot. In the confusion, Lincoln would be either shot or stabbed.

Pinkerton said, "We propose to take you on to Washington this very night, Mr. President, and steal a march on your enemies."

Lincoln doubted that the plot was real and serious. Pinkerton, sure that danger lay ahead, desperately tried to convince the president, but without success. After listening thoughtfully to Pinkerton, Lincoln said, "Tomorrow morning I have promised to raise the flag over Independence Hall. After that to visit the legislature in Harrisburg. Whatever the cost, these two promises I must fulfill."[10]

So Pinkerton's plan to race on to Washington was rejected. The detective almost lost hope of preventing assassination in Baltimore. Lincoln, it seemed, might not live to serve as president of the United States.

Detective Pinkerton spent a worried evening at the Continental Hotel, where the president and his group were staying. He and Ward Hill Lamon tried to keep a close watch on Lincoln, but it was difficult as the president mingled with his guests.

The hotel ballroom and banquet rooms were gaily decorated with flags and streamers. The party was aptly called "jollification for Mr. Lincoln."[1] The ballroom was packed with waltzing couples, the women wearing bell-shaped hoop skirts. A band played a serenade. Hundreds of Philadelphia's leading citizens had come to salute Lincoln on his way to Washington.

Lincoln's eldest son, Robert, helped greet the guests. A student at Harvard, he had been excused from his college classes to join his family for the trip to Washington. Young Robert Lincoln had become famous during the past year. The heir to the British throne, the Prince of Wales, had recently paid a visit to the United States. Now the newspapers nicknamed Robert Lincoln the "Prince of Rails" because of all the publicity about his father's youthful work as a rail-splitter.[2] Robert,

4

LIKE A THIEF IN THE NIGHT

along with a few others, had been told about the Baltimore plot, and he, too, was worried.

Lincoln himself, however, showed no sign of concern as he shook hands with countless well-wishers, smiling and telling some of the stories for which he was famous.

Meanwhile, a train was speeding northward from Washington to Philadelphia. On board was a messenger bringing urgent and secret news for Lincoln.

The messenger was Frederick W. Seward, the son of William Seward, whom Lincoln had recently chosen to become secretary of state. William Seward was a leading Republican and a senator from the state of New York. That morning, Senator Seward had been in the Senate chamber when an army officer came to him with an alarming report about the Baltimore plot to murder Lincoln.

The senator realized that Lincoln must be warned at once but was puzzled about how to get word to him. He did not trust the telegraph service, since operators did not always keep messages confidential. He could not go himself because of the crisis taking place in the country. In the South, preparations were underway to inaugurate Jefferson Davis as the first president of the Confederacy. Clearly, the country was breaking up. William Seward, who had recently been described as the only calm man in the Senate, did not dare leave Washington at such a time.[3]

Senator William Seward was on the Senate floor when he learned about the Baltimore plot. He became Lincoln's secretary of state and is chiefly remembered today for the purchase of Alaska.

Then he remembered that his son Frederick was in the gallery that morning. He called Frederick down to the Senate floor.

"I want you to go by the first train," Seward told Frederick. "Find Mr. Lincoln wherever he is. Let no one else know your errand."[4]

A Secret Message

Young Frederick arrived at the Philadelphia depot at 10:00 P.M. and raced to the Continental Hotel. A huge party was in progress, but he found Robert Lincoln at the main staircase and explained it was urgent for him to see the president in private.

There was no way to speak privately at the party. Ward Hill Lamon, who was also there, said to Frederick, "I'd better take you to his bedroom. He has to got to go there sometime tonight. It is the only place I know of where he will be likely to be alone."[5]

Frederick waited impatiently for more than an hour in Lincoln's bedroom, listening to the noise of the party outside the door. At last, Lincoln came in. Frederick, who had never seen the president before, thought he looked just like his portraits, but the pictures "omitted his careworn look, and his pleasant, kindly smile."[6]

Lincoln read the letters Frederick had brought, holding them up to the gaslight in the dim hotel room. Then he questioned Frederick closely about how these reports had been obtained.

At last, Lincoln nodded slowly and told Frederick about Allan Pinkerton's warning, saying, "Only today, since we arrived at this house, he brought this story about an attempt on my life in the confusion and hurly-burly of the reception at Baltimore."

"Surely, Mr. Lincoln," said Seward, "that is strong corroboration of the news I bring you."[7]

Lincoln smiled. "That is exactly why I was asking you about names. If different persons, not knowing of each other's work, pursue clues that led to the same result, it shows there may be something in it."[8]

Frederick urged Lincoln to change his travel plans, but Lincoln rose, saying, "Well, we haven't got to decide it tonight anyway. I see it is getting late."[9]

Lincoln noticed that young Seward seemed disappointed in his slowness to make a decision. Then, in a kindly voice, Lincoln said, "You need not think I will not consider it well. I shall think it over carefully and try to decide it right. I will let you know in the morning."[10]

Frederick Seward, son of Senator William Seward, carried a warning to Lincoln in Philadelphia. Frederick later served as assistant secretary of state.

Actually, there was a great deal for Lincoln to think over. The country needed a strong, courageous leader. How would it look if he changed his plans because of an empty threat? Would he seem cowardly?

Yet there seemed to be no denying that a murder plot existed. Different detectives, working separately, had now reported it. Also, Lincoln had to think about matters in the city of Baltimore and the state of Maryland. The governor of the state was trying to keep Maryland in the Union. But rebels had threatened his life and announced that they would attack any Union troops that crossed the state. They might even march to Washington and seize the city.

Lincoln Chooses Caution

Early the next morning, February 22, Lincoln attended ceremonies honoring George Washington's birthday. He spoke to a crowd in Independence Hall. Something he said in that speech showed that he had been thinking deeply about the Baltimore plot. He spoke of the ideals of equality in the Declaration of Independence. He said that if the country could be saved with those ideals, he "would be one of the happiest men in the world. But if it cannot be saved without giving up that principle, I would rather be assassinated on this spot than surrender it."[11]

Later, Frederick Seward met Lincoln in the hotel lobby and was told that the president would change his plans regarding his arrival in Baltimore. Seward then hurried to the telegraph office to send his father a message in a secret code they had worked out.

At 5:45 P.M. on February 22, Lincoln sat down at a dinner table in a hotel, the Jones House in Harrisburg. Then he quietly told his friends of his new plans. Not all of them agreed. One man, an army colonel, said he would "Get a squad of cavalry, sir, and *cut* our way to Washington!"[12]

Lincoln himself was still concerned, wondering "What would the nation think of its president stealing into its capital like a thief in the night?"[13]

But the plan was set. Lincoln left the table and went to his upstairs room. He put on a traveling suit and carried a soft felt hat and a folded shawl.

A few minutes later, he and Lamon were in a closed carriage rolling briskly to the railway station. There they boarded a train especially arranged by the Pennsylvania Railroad to carry only their own car. At the same time, all the telegraph lines from Harrisburg were cut, so news of the president's departure could not leak out.

This special train took them to Philadelphia, where, in the darkness, they were met by Detective Pinkerton. One of Pinkerton's detectives, a woman, had reserved berths in a sleeping car, including one for her "invalid brother."[14] The "invalid," actually Lincoln, was smuggled into the berth, and the curtains were tightly drawn.

Ward Hill Lamon occupied the next berth. He had brought along two ordinary pistols, two special derringer pistols, and two big knives.[15]

They arrived in Baltimore at 3:30 A.M., when the whole city seemed to be asleep. Pinkerton wrote in his diary, "Darkness and silence reigned over all . . . Our presence in Baltimore was entirely unsuspected."[16]

They changed trains safely. Yet Lincoln and Lamon were not exactly unnoticeable. They were almost a pair of giants, one standing six feet four inches, and the other six feet two inches.

Soon the new train was hurrying on toward Washington. The Baltimore plotters had been outfoxed.

At six o'clock in the morning, as the train arrived in the nation's capital, Allan Pinkerton sent a telegram to the head of the Pennsylvania Railroad that read:

PLUMS DELIVERED NUTS SAFELY[17]

This was another code. It meant that the president was safe in Washington at last.

Lincoln's arrival was not quite what he had feared. He did not come skulking in "like a thief in the night."[18] But, when he stepped from the train to the platform, there was no throng of well-wishers, no band music, not the least ceremony of welcome. It was the strangest entrance a president had ever made into his nation's capital.

Abraham Lincoln had escaped the Baltimore plotters, but he did not escape the newspapers. As soon as word leaked out about his secret journey, editors began to ridicule the new president.

Because of one false report, the press had the mistaken idea that Lincoln had worn a full disguise. Supposedly, he had put on a Scottish plaid cap with long streamers, and a coat that fell to his ankles. This was not true, but it made a good story.

THE THREATENED CAPITAL

Vanity Fair magazine ran a cartoon of Lincoln dressed in a full Scottish costume, including a kilt, and dancing the Highland fling. In Baltimore, the city where the trouble had started, a newspaper showed Lincoln sneaking out of a freight car.[1]

Often, the words written about Lincoln were as cruel as the drawings. In Louisville, Kentucky, the *Courier* said, "Lincoln runs for his life . . . and leaves his wife. They ought to swap clothes . . . Lincoln began the exchange by assuming her striped petticoat . . ."[2]

Several newspapers claimed that Lincoln had been in no real danger. They pointed out that there was no solid proof of the Baltimore plot, only people's opinions.

Many newspapers printed cartoons mocking Lincoln's secret trip from Harrisburg to Washington. It was falsely said that he arrived in his wife's clothes.

No one can know for sure whether the Baltimore plot was real. We do know, however, what happened later when a train that *might* have carried Lincoln arrived in Baltimore. The incident proved that there was danger to the new president. The *Baltimore Sun* described the scene:

> As soon as the train stopped, the crowd leaped upon the platforms and mounted to the tops of the cars like so many monkeys . . . like a hive of bees they swarmed upon them, shouting, hallooing, and making all manner of noise.[3]

The press was quite wrong in accusing Lincoln of being cowardly. Although he did not foolishly go out to look for danger, he refused most special precautions.

He did not want extra guards, he would not avoid public appearances, and he seemed forgetful of caution. Lincoln's friends almost despaired of shielding him from his enemies.

Yet there was danger on every side in Washington, D.C. The people of the city were mostly Southern, at least as much as the people of Baltimore and almost as much as the citizens of Richmond. Their loyalty was to the new nation now being formed, the Confederate States of America. In some places, the shooting that would become the Civil War had already begun. Feelings ran deep and violent in the capital, with many people blaming Lincoln for the coming bloodshed.

In Lincoln's time, Washington, D.C., was not the beautiful city it is today. The new Capitol Building stood unfinished, lacking a dome and some walls. Most streets were long stretches of mud or dust, depending on the time of year. There were no sewers or paved gutters. Plans to create majestic structures had been halted by the nation's troubles. Scattered in the center of Washington lay heaps and stacks of stone blocks, sheet metal, and lumber. All these building materials would remain unused for years.

The city had a population of slightly more than sixty thousand. About three thousand of these people were slaves. There were four times as many African-American freedmen as slaves. These free African Americans, many of whom were women, were former slaves or children of slaves who had legally gained their freedom. Many of the Southerners in the city had a special hatred for the free African Americans. Perhaps they saw in them an omen for the future. This added tension to an already troubled and divided city.

Gangs often roamed the streets unchecked. There were only fifty policemen paid by the city to patrol in daylight. Another fifty officers were in charge at night, but they were employees of the federal government, and their duty was mainly to guard public buildings. One historian has written, "It was a courageous man who ventured to walk alone by night in the ill-lighted streets of the capital of the United States."[4]

Inauguration in an Armed Capital

The city bristled with guns and bayonets on March 4, 1861, the day of Lincoln's inauguration. Army sharpshooters were posted on roofs along Pennsylvania Avenue where Lincoln and outgoing President James Buchanan would pass. Spectators lining the streets talked of rebel plots to seize the city, saying there would be an uprising before Lincoln took office. Or, if not that, Southern troops would ride over the Long Bridge from Virginia in the evening to seize President Lincoln at the inaugural ball.

Heavy artillery was poised on a hilltop overlooking the Capitol, and new cannon emplacements commanded the Potomac River.

Early in the afternoon, Lincoln and Buchanan appeared in an open carriage. Lincoln had insisted that the carriage be open, not closed. Its iron-rimmed wheels ground over the cobblestoned street.

Few people had a good view of Lincoln. A troop of mounted soldiers escorted the coach. The officer commanding them kept spurring his horse to make it uneasy. This affected all the horses nearby. The officer hoped the jerking, shifting movements of the horses would make it difficult for any marksman to aim at Lincoln.

Lincoln, in a new black suit and silk stovepipe hat, mounted a speaker's platform in front of the Capitol. Under the platform, fifty guards stood ready for trouble while sharpshooters watched from every nearby window.

As he prepared to speak, Lincoln seemed uncertain about what to do with his tall hat. His old opponent, Stephen Douglas, was sitting among the officials on the platform. Smiling, he took Lincoln's hat and held

SOURCE DOCUMENT

I AM LOATH TO CLOSE. WE ARE NOT ENEMIES, BUT FRIENDS. WE MUST NOT BE ENEMIES. THOUGH PASSION MAY HAVE STRAINED, IT MUST NOT BREAK OUR BONDS OF AFFECTION. THE MYSTIC CHORDS OF MEMORY, STRETCHING FROM EVERY BATTLEFIELD AND PATRIOT GRAVE TO EVERY LIVING HEART AND HEARTHSTONE ALL OVER THIS BROAD LAND, WILL YET SWELL THE CHORUS OF THE UNION, WHEN AGAIN TOUCHED, AS SURELY THEY WILL BE, BY THE BETTER ANGELS OF OUR NATURE.[5]

In his first inaugural address, President Lincoln urged the people of the nation to overcome their differences in order to preserve the union of the states.

it for the next half hour while Lincoln officially became president of the United States.

So, under heavy guard, Abraham Lincoln took office, delivering a speech that claimed the states were "friends, not enemies."[6] His words were eloquent, but only a little over a month later, cannons were roaring in the harbor of Charleston, South Carolina, firing at a United States military base called Fort Sumter. The Civil War had started.

The President Seems an Easy Target

Today it seems astonishing that in Lincoln's time the president had so little daily protection, especially in wartime. Dozens of tourists and sightseers freely wandered into the White House, making themselves at home. Some, easily getting past the one guard, even entered the Lincolns' private living quarters. No one was questioned or searched for weapons.

Almost every day, especially during his early months as president, men seeking government jobs came into Lincoln's office. He also talked to such men in the halls of the White House, on the stairway, on the front steps, even at times in the streets of Washington, where they would approach him. Lincoln's worry was that these office seekers took up so much of his time. He did not seem to think that any of these visitors might be armed and dangerous. But Lamon and Secretary of War Edwin Stanton realized Lincoln's peril.

Many historians feel that at the time, the United States government had two main tasks: destroying the Confederacy and preserving the life of President Lincoln.

The first task, winning the war, seemed easy to some Northerners early in 1861. But they were quickly shocked into understanding how serious the situation was. The struggle would continue for four brutal years.

Only a week after the war began in the harbor of Charleston, South Carolina, rebel sympathizers in Maryland seized and burned railroad bridges. Suddenly, Washington, D.C., was cut off from the rest of the nation. It was like an island ringed by a sea of enemies.

The people of Washington closed their shutters and huddled indoors. Rumors of attacks by Southern armies and uprisings of local mobs alarmed the city. It was said that Lincoln and his Cabinet would be arrested and taken South. Perhaps they would all be shot!

The handful of loyal army officers in Washington rushed to prepare a desperate defense. The Treasury Building was barricaded. Boards, stones, and kegs of cement blocked the doors and windows of the Capitol. Iron plates intended for the new dome now became armor for the entrance.

Throughout the ordeal, Lincoln seemed calm while others panicked. Yet he was under a terrible strain. One day, he said he heard nearby cannon fire, although no one else in the White House heard it. Lincoln went outside to investigate and walked a distance to the government arsenal, where arms and ammunition were stored. The doors of the arsenal stood open and the guards had deserted their posts, leaving the stacks of weapons unprotected. Lincoln summoned new guards.

The president had only imagined the sound of cannon fire. But he had seen for himself what poor protection Washington offered.

Fortunately, trains from the North were soon running again, and troops arrived to reinforce the city. The immediate danger was over.

Lincoln's Protector, Edwin Stanton

The Cabinet officer responsible for Lincoln's safety was the secretary of war. During the first ten months of Lincoln's first term, this position was held by Simon Cameron, a political boss from Pennsylvania. In January 1862, Cameron was replaced by Edwin M. Stanton.

Stanton, considered one of the best lawyers in the country, was a capable manager and organizer, but a difficult personality. His short temper and sharp tongue were feared and hated by many. When he first met Lincoln, he felt a "sneering contempt" for Lincoln's awkwardness and simplicity.[7] In one letter, he even referred to Lincoln as "the original gorilla."[8] Gradually, through the years of the Civil War, he developed a great respect for Lincoln. Always he did his best to protect the president.

Stanton was deeply troubled about the number of Confederate sympathizers in Washington, D.C. He suspected that many of them were spies, and some might be dangerous to the president. As the war

Edwin M. Stanton, secretary of war, took threats against the president seriously. Lincoln's carelessness about safety made Stanton's task a difficult one.

UNITED STATES OF AMERICA

THIRTY SIXTH CONGRESS

Washington City 30th Jany 1861

Your note is rec'd – Believe me or not you cannot be more wretched than I am. I cannot now explain. Let it suffice until we meet: that for the last few days every movement and act of mine have been watched with Hawkeyed vigilance. For your sake more than my own I have been compelled to be cautious: But tomorrow at 10 A M I will see you at all hazzards –

Yours &c
H

This letter, written on official paper of the Congress, was found in the home of Confederate spy Rose Greenhow. The writer, who also may have been a spy, has never been identified.

continued, Stanton compiled lists of people he suspected were traitors to the Union. Many were thrown in jail with little regard for their rights or the law. Most were innocent, but a few proved to be real Confederate agents working undercover.

The most famous of the spies Stanton imprisoned was a woman, Rose O'Neal Greenhow. Living in Washington, Greenhow sent messages to the Confederate Army about military matters. Information from Greenhow helped the South win a victory in the first Battle of Bull Run. Several other women were also charged with spying and imprisoned for a time.

Detective Allan Pinkerton worked closely with Stanton in investigating Confederate plots in Washington. He moved his entire detective agency from Chicago to Washington for wartime operations.

But there was one name that neither Pinkerton nor Stanton had on the long list of suspects. The man they should have been watching closely was John Wilkes Booth. He was among America's foremost stage actors and would one day prove to be the most dangerous man in Washington.

6

THE MAN WHO HATED LINCOLN

Abraham Lincoln had always enjoyed going to the theater. Spending an evening watching fictional events on the stage gave him relief from the pressure of his duties. As the Civil War worsened, he needed such an escape from worry and strain. Despite his heavy duties, he managed to see several plays each year.

The president's love of the stage caused some criticism. Many churches and ministers condemned all playhouses as wicked haunts of the devil. Plays, these religious leaders insisted, were always evil, and actors were immoral. Lincoln ignored this view and continued to take pleasure in the theater. He especially loved the works of William Shakespeare and could quote long passages of Shakespeare from memory.

Mrs. Lincoln always went with him. She enjoyed plays and other literary pursuits. Besides, going to the theater gave her a chance to enjoy the attention she received as the president's wife. She spent large amounts of money and even went into debt for fashionable clothes. At the theater, she could show off her wardrobe.

The Lincolns often invited friends to share the presidential box at Grover's Theatre or at the other new and elegant playhouse, Ford's. Usually, the theater managers had the orchestra play "Hail to the Chief" when the Lincolns entered, and the audience stood to applaud. Mary Todd Lincoln loved such flattering recognition.

Secretary of War Stanton felt uneasy about Lincoln's attendance at plays because it was almost impossible to protect the president in a huge crowd. Ford's Theatre could seat almost seventeen hundred, and dangerous people could easily join the audience.

Lincoln ignored Stanton's advice, just as he ignored the complaining clergymen. The theater remained a place of relaxation and refuge for him in a time of terrible stress. He occupied the presidential box at Ford's at least twelve times.

One night there was serious trouble. The Lincolns had gone to Grover's Theatre with a political friend, Schuyler Colfax, the speaker of the House of Representatives. Lincoln was supposed to have a cavalry escort for such outings, but as usual he preferred to go without it.

Danger at Grover's Theatre

Grover's Theatre was near a rough neighborhood of saloons frequented by Southern sympathizers. This particular week, they were especially angry because Lincoln had just signed the Emancipation Proclamation, which freed most of the slaves. In the streets, troublemakers had hurled stones and insults at African Americans. Even church services were disrupted by protests. Such was the mood in Washington that night when Lincoln went unguarded to the theater.

After the performance, when the Lincolns entered their carriage, their coachman was drunk. He fell on the sidewalk, unable to drive. Meanwhile, an ugly mob gathered, jeering and threatening the president.

The mood of the crowd alarmed Leonard Grover, owner of the theater. He leaped to the driver's seat of the carriage and urged the horses forward, leaving the shouting, cursing mob behind.

Usually, no violence marred such evenings. So it was on the night of April 9, 1863, when the Lincolns went to Ford's Theatre to see a melodrama called *The Marble Heart*. The story involved the romantic adventures of a sculptor and was full of violent action. Lincoln dismissed the play as nonsense, and later his secretary, John Hay, said that it was "Rather tame than otherwise."[1]

Since it was not the kind of play the president enjoyed, it seems possible that the Lincolns attended because a famous young actor was appearing for the first time at Ford's Theatre. This star, the youngest brother in a great theatrical family, was said to be "the handsomest man in America."[2] Onstage, he surprised and delighted audiences with his athletic feats—leaps from high platforms, sword play, and combat scenes.

That night was probably the only time Lincoln ever saw that actor—whose name was John Wilkes Booth.

Background of an Assassin

When "Johnnie" Wilkes Booth was about fourteen years old, a gypsy fortune-teller read his palm. He had, she declared, "a bad hand." In fact, she had never seen a worse one.

"You were born under an unlucky star," she told him. "I see a thundering crowd of enemies, and not one friend. You will die young and make a bad end."[3]

Most people would just shrug off such a prediction as foolish, as mere superstition or guesswork. But young Johnnie believed the words and was frightened. Booth's sister, Asia, would say that later in life the actor was often troubled and worried by these dark predictions. His sister thought his fears made him determined to "perform some deed that would make his name live forever."[4]

Booth's former schoolmates later declared the same thing. One said that Booth wanted to "do something . . . so he would never be forgotten, even after he had been dead a thousand years."[5]

Booth was born in Maryland, an area divided in sympathy between friends and opponents of slavery, between North and South. His father, Junius Brutus Booth, was widely considered one of the greatest Shakespearean actors of his generation. As a youth, John's elder brother, Edwin Booth, showed great talent as a classical actor. Eventually, Edwin surpassed his father. Another brother, named for his father, Junius Brutus Booth, also successfully joined the ranks of professional actors.

Young Johnnie displayed childhood athletic ability, becoming a fine horseman and a crack pistol shot. At seventeen, he began a career as a professional actor, thrilling audiences with his skilled fencing and graceful movement. But early in his career he was careless about memorizing his lines and sometimes forgot the words he was supposed to say. Audiences responded in the manner of the day: They hissed at him.

Booth's handsome features, talent, and strong voice helped him rise to stardom, mostly in plays packed with violence and murder. Several times, he was slashed during duels on stage. He would continue fighting with blood streaming down his face.

In 1860, he earned thirty thousand dollars as an actor, a very impressive income at the time, far more than most lawyers or doctors earned.

From the beginning of the Civil War, Booth was a strong supporter of the South, mostly because of his staunch belief in slavery. He once wrote to his brother-in-law that slavery was "one of the greatest blessings . . . that God had ever bestowed upon a favored nation."[6]

Although outspoken in his enthusiasm for the Southern cause, Booth never actually joined the Confederate Army. Still, he aided the cause of the South in other ways. The Northern blockade of Southern seaports caused many shortages in the South. Booth smuggled medicines, such as quinine, to the Confederates. At times, he also served as a spy.

Booth's love of the South seems less deep than his dedication to slavery and his hatred of African

This is one of John Wilkes Booth's favorite photos of himself. The actor was horrified by the idea of freedom for the slaves. He hoped to win glory by performing a bold deed for the South.

Americans. One historian has explained, "John Wilkes Booth was not a madman, was not a drunk, and was not a failed actor in search of glory."[7] Above all, he was a man filled with deep racial hatred.

Plotting Against the President

In the autumn of 1864, when the war was going badly for the South, Booth devised a daring plan. With the help of several other men who were devoted to the South, he would kidnap Lincoln and carry him into Virginia. Lincoln's captors would then demand the release of all Southern prisoners of war in exchange for the president.

During the next few months, Booth found six helpers to carry out this plan. The plotters were: Michael O'Laughlin and Samuel Arnold, who had been Booth's schoolmates and had both served briefly in the Confederate Army; George Atzerodt, a wagon maker from Maryland; nineteen-year-old David Herold, who had worked as a clerk in a Washington drugstore; twenty-year-old Lewis Powell, who some-times called himself Lewis Paine and had earlier deserted from the Confederate Army; and John H. Surratt, a secret messenger for the Confederacy, whose mother, Mary Surratt, had recently moved to Washington from Maryland to open a boardinghouse.

The plotters met several times in Mrs. Surratt's house, and stored weapons there. It is uncertain, though, how much Mary Surratt actually knew of their plans.

Booth learned that Lincoln was to visit the Soldiers' Home, a hospital at the edge of the city, on March 16, 1865. Along the road were clumps of trees that would provide cover for an ambush. Booth's gang, heavily armed with knives and pistols, waited in a grove to pounce on Lincoln when his carriage passed. Hours went by but the presidential carriage never appeared. At last, Booth gave up and the armed men headed back to the city. Why, they wondered, had Lincoln suddenly changed his plans? Perhaps their plot had been discovered. The conspirators quickly separated to avoid capture.

Two of them, Arnold and O'Laughlin, went back to Baltimore and had nothing further to do with Booth's plans. Much later, when the two men claimed this in a court of law, no one believed them.

It soon became apparent to the rest of the gang that the plot had not been detected. Lincoln had simply changed his plans and had been saved by luck.

Booth Grows Desperate

Every passing day made it clearer that the war was drawing to a close and that the Union was winning. If Booth was to strike a blow for the South, it would have to be soon. Meanwhile, things were happening to deepen his hatred of the president.

Richmond, the capital of the Confederacy, had fallen. Lincoln made a quick trip there to see the ruins of the city that had held out so long against the Northern armies. Lincoln had hardly stepped ashore

Lincoln's Emancipation Proclamation freed the slaves in the states of the rebellious Confederacy. These former slaves have somehow found horses and a wagon and are fleeing northward from the war. Freeing the slaves deepened Booth's hatred of Lincoln.

from the river steamer when he was surrounded by a crowd of African Americans who had been slaves only a few days earlier. The crowd cheered and shouted. A man who was with Lincoln that day later wrote, "They would not feel they were free in reality until they heard it from his own lips."[8]

Lincoln said to them, "You are free—free as air. You can cast off the name of slave and trample upon it . . . Liberty is your birthright . . . It is a sin you have been deprived of it for so many years."[9]

Such words were more than enough to inflame John Wilkes Booth. Soon Lincoln would say things Booth considered even worse.

On the night of April 11, 1865, Abraham Lincoln gave what would prove to be his last public speech. Booth and his helpers Paine and Herold were in the crowd outside the White House. Booth listened with growing horror as Lincoln spoke of granting former slaves some voting rights.

His companions heard Booth say, "Now, by God, I'll put him through! That is the last speech he will ever make!"[10]

Soon afterward, Booth would write in his diary, "Something decisive must be done."[11]

Plans for kidnapping had changed to plans for murder.

7

BOOTH: SETTING THE STAGE FOR MURDER

On Good Friday, April 14, 1865, while many Washington residents thought about religious services, John Wilkes Booth hurried to make final arrangements for his "decisive" act.

Over the last few days, the plan had taken shape in his mind. It was a daring and ambitious project. Booth intended to assassinate not only Abraham Lincoln but also the two most prominent figures in the government of the United States.

He intended to leave the country leaderless. The confusion that would follow, he hoped, would benefit the South. Booth had made up a death list that contained three names: Abraham Lincoln, Vice President Andrew Johnson, and Secretary of State William Seward. Many Americans believed that the secretary of state, as the senior Cabinet officer, was second in line to succeed the president. This was not actually the law, but it is possible that Booth thought it was.

Booth had already assigned the roles his followers were to play. Lewis Paine, an experienced fighter hardened by war, would murder William Seward.

George Atzerodt was to shoot the vice president. David Herold, considered "light and trifling," was trusted only with guiding Paine to Seward's house.[1]

After having breakfast at the National Hotel, where he was staying, Booth went to a barber shop, and then to Grover's Theatre. That night, an elaborate production of *The Thousand and One Nights* tale, "Aladdin," would light up the stage, and Booth knew that the Lincolns had been invited. He did not know if they had accepted. Booth went next to Kirkwood House, the hotel where Vice President Andrew Johnson was living. During the war, it had been necessary to have a special pass to cross the bridge from Washington into the enemy state of Virginia. It is likely that Booth went to Kirkwood House to ask the vice president to sign such a pass. Booth apparently did not know that the rule had been recently relaxed—passes were no longer needed.

Andrew Johnson was not in, so Booth left a brief note for Johnson's secretary, then went on his way. He paused briefly at the National Hotel, then continued on to the boardinghouse of Mary Surratt.

The Surratt House—A Nest of Spies

Mary Surratt's house on H Street had long been a center of rebel plotting and espionage, or spying. Most of Booth's conspiracy had been hatched there. Surratt, a widow, had inherited a tavern at a Maryland crossroads called Surrattsville. A few years earlier, she had leased the tavern so she could move to Washington with her son, John, and her young daughter, Anna. John often rode his horse through the night to deliver secret letters for the Confederacy. The boardinghouse in Washington was drab and ordinary, a place for low-paid government clerks and workers.

When Booth arrived there on the morning of April 14, he knew Mrs. Surratt was going to make a quick trip to Surrattsville later. He may have asked her to find out about army guard posts along the road he planned to travel that night.

Booth went next to Ford's Theatre. It was about noon. As he entered, Harry Clay Ford, the theater treasurer, exclaimed, "There comes the handsomest man in Washington."[2] Booth was a friend of the management, so he received his mail at the theater and had free access at any time.

Booth learned that the president and Mrs. Lincoln would be attending *Our American Cousin* that evening. The official box had been opened and was being decorated. Edward Spangler, a carpenter who had worked for Booth's family years before, was now a stagehand at the playhouse. He probably spoke to Booth, since they were old friends. Spangler was taking down a partition to enlarge the presidential box. Booth was told that more space was needed because General Ulysses S. Grant and his wife, Julia Dent Grant, would be sharing the box with the Lincolns.

To tease Booth, Harry Clay Ford said jokingly, "Jefferson Davis and Robert E. Lee will also be here—captives in another box."[3]

Booth was in no mood for jokes. He denounced Lee for surrendering to Grant at Appomattox Court House.

Knowing now where the Lincolns would be that evening, Booth went ahead with his arrangements. First, he went to Pumphery's Stable near the National Hotel. He wanted to rent a saddle horse and have it ready at 4:00 that afternoon. "Don't give me any but a good one," he insisted.[4] He expected to need a strong, fast mount that night.

Not far from the stable was the Willard Hotel, where General Grant and his wife were staying. That was Booth's next stop.

Mrs. Grant and her young son Jesse were having lunch in the hotel dining room. A man "with a wild look" entered, sat down at a nearby table, and watched her with a flat, unblinking stare.[5] When she spoke to her son, the man cocked his head, trying to listen. The general's wife was becoming truly alarmed when the man suddenly left. Mrs. Grant later identified the man as Booth.[6]

Booth tried again to see Vice President Johnson about getting a pass to travel south that night. But Johnson was not in his room at Kirkwood House. He had an appointment with President Lincoln.

At Ford's Theatre

It was now mid-afternoon, about 2:30, and Booth returned to the Surratt boardinghouse to give Mary Surratt a package to leave for him at the tavern in

Surrattsville. It contained binoculars, which he probably thought would be useful during his escape.

A little later, Booth was back at Ford's Theatre, where a rehearsal of *Our American Cousin* had just finished. The actors were leaving, but a quartet was practicing a special song, "Honor to Our Soldiers," to be sung that night as a tribute to President Lincoln and General Grant. Flags were being arranged on the presidential box.

The management of the theater was busy getting out word that Lincoln and Grant would be attending *Our American Cousin* that night. Special handbills and advertisements were being printed. Here was a chance to fill the house for a play that was not first-rate and had a star, Laura Keene, who was past her greatest fame. For the theater company, the attendance of the country's two greatest heroes was a wonderful stroke of luck. They would sell almost every seat.

The presidential box at Ford's was really two boxes that could be combined into one quite large space. The decoration was elegant, with figured wallpaper of deep red, and rich Turkish carpet. English lace curtains overhung with yellow satin draperies gave the occupants privacy.

To reach the box, it was necessary to walk behind the seats of the lowest balcony, which was the dress circle, then go down a little private hallway about ten feet long. Spectators in the theater could see anyone coming or going. This lack of a private entrance had caused Booth's friends to reject a plan the actor had once urged to kidnap Lincoln during a performance. It was an impossible scheme. There was no way out of the box except through the audience or across the stage eleven feet below.

The theater had originally been the First Baptist Church of Washington. John T. Ford of Baltimore bought the building when the congregation decided to move to a more fashionable neighborhood. Dark predictions were made at the time: It would be bad luck to turn a church into a playhouse. Disaster would follow!

These predictions seemed true when a faulty meter for gaslights caused a fire on New Year's Eve, 1862.

Laura Keene, star of Our American Cousin, *became the first woman theatrical manager in the United States. On April 14, 1865, she helped calm the audience after Lincoln was shot.*

The presidential box at Ford's was lavishly decorated with five flags and a picture of George Washington. But few precautions had been taken to protect the president's safety.

Only the blackened walls were left standing. But the rebuilt theater was now prospering. No one expected further bad luck.

Booth watched workers put finishing touches on the presidential box. He then continued to prepare for what he thought would be the greatest night of his life. Back at the National Hotel, Booth wrote a letter, put it in his coat pocket, and went on his way. He picked up a fine, spirited mare at the livery stable and rode it in the streets of Washington. He showed off its gait and his own riding skill, boasting that his mount could "Run like a cat!"[7]

In the street, he greeted John Matthews, an actor playing in *Our American Cousin*. "Perhaps I may leave town tonight," said Booth. "I have a letter here which I desire to be published in the *National Intelligencer*. Please attend to it for me."[8]

As Matthews accepted the letter, he noticed a coach passing rapidly. "Why, there goes Grant," he said. "I thought he was coming to the theater with the president this evening."[9]

Booth set off at a gallop after the coach. When he was passing it, he leaned toward the window to peer inside.

Mrs. Grant, sitting beside her husband, exclaimed that it was the same man she had seen during lunch. She said, "I don't like his looks!"[10]

Booth watched the carriage turn toward the railroad depot. He learned a few minutes later that the Grants were leaving for New Jersey at once and would not go to the theater that night.

General Ulysses S. Grant, Northern commander and later president of the United States, was marked for death by Booth. Luckily, he and his wife decided not to join the Lincolns at the theater.

"The Most Talked About Man in America"

Booth appeared again at Ford's after leaving the mare at a stable behind the theater. He invited some acquaintances he met at Ford's to join him for a drink in the restaurant next door. He left them at 5:00 P.M.

It is not known what John Wilkes Booth did during the next hour. For years, it was believed that he went back to the theater and bored a peephole in the door of the box Lincoln would occupy. He might also have arranged a wooden wedge to hold another door shut behind him. Now it seems he did neither of these things. The tiny peephole that puzzled investigators had been cut long before so a guard could protect the president. A board wedged against the wall had been used to fasten the door because the lock was broken.[11]

About 6:30 P.M., Booth went to his room at the hotel, probably to get the weapons he planned to use that night.

William Withers, director of the orchestra at Ford's, happened to meet Booth and they had a drink together. Withers, teasing Booth, remarked that John Wilkes would never be as great an actor as his father.

Booth replied with a mysterious smile, saying, "When I leave the stage, I will be the most talked about man in America."[12]

Withers thought Booth was simply bragging. Later on, he remembered the remark "with shock."[13]

At about 8:00 P.M., Booth went to another hotel, Herndon House. There he met with his fellow

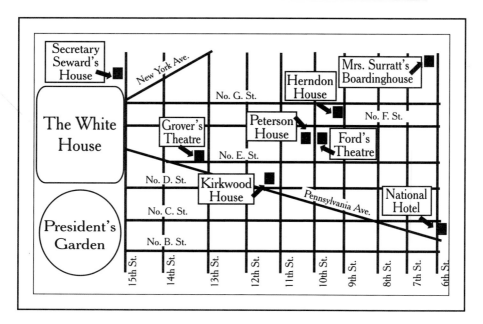

*All the main events of the assassination of Lincoln took place
inside a small area in the middle of Washington, D.C.*

plotters. In this secret meeting, the plans for that night
were reviewed. It was settled that Booth would shoot
Lincoln. Lewis Paine would kill Secretary of State
Seward with a knife. George Atzerodt had the job of
assassinating Vice President Johnson. Everything was
ready for the violent events to come.

A DREAM HAUNTS ABRAHAM LINCOLN

Early in April 1865, a little more than a week before the terrible night in Ford's Theatre, President Lincoln and his wife were chatting with a few friends at the White House. One of the guests was Ward Hill Lamon, Lincoln's old friend from Illinois. Lamon had made himself Lincoln's unofficial bodyguard almost five years before.

To Lamon, Lincoln seemed unusually sad and serious that evening. He remarked that he had recently been disturbed by a troubling dream. This dream had come to him several nights earlier, but the memory still haunted him.[1]

Mary Todd Lincoln asked her husband if he believed in dreams. Lincoln replied that he did not. Still, he had taken this one so seriously that he had even made notes about it after awakening.

Mrs. Lincoln, although insisting she did not think dreams had any meaning, demanded that her husband tell her about his. Her curiosity was aroused.

Lincoln agreed at last and spoke slowly, with sadness. He said that he had gone to bed very late about ten days before. He had had a stressful day, waiting for news from the battlefront. When he fell asleep, he began to dream that everything around him was extremely silent, and that people somewhere nearby were crying. He explained, "I thought I left my bed and wandered downstairs. There was silence broken by the same pitiful sobbing. But the mourners were invisible. I went from room to room, but no living person was in sight."

Lincoln said that he at last entered the large East Room of the White House, where he saw a coffin and a corpse laid out for burial. Some soldiers stood on guard nearby, and Lincoln asked them who had died.

A soldier told him it was the president, who had been killed by an assassin.

Then the weeping of the mourners seemed so loud that it woke Lincoln, freeing him from his dream.

"I slept no more that night," he told his guests. "Although it was only a dream, I have been strangely annoyed by it ever since."

"That is horrid!" Mrs. Lincoln exclaimed, "I am glad I don't believe in dreams!"

Lincoln tried to make light of what he had just told her. He cracked a joke, and he told Lamon there was no reason to be afraid.[2]

Years afterward, some historians would doubt the whole story of the dream, saying it came from Lamon's imagination. Others have felt it was true. True or exaggerated, the dream has become an unforgettable part of the story of Abraham Lincoln.

The Last Days

Washington was celebrating the end of the Civil War, and most people did not think much about danger to Lincoln. But Lamon continued to be concerned. At Lincoln's request, he was going on a mission to Richmond on April 12. For a few days, he would not be on hand to guard his friend.

He tried but failed to make Lincoln promise not to go out at night. "Especially to the theater," he pleaded. But Lincoln would not promise. Lamon's fears, he said, were "nonsense."[3]

Good Friday, April 14, 1865, was a working day for Lincoln. At 7:00 A.M., he rose in his second-floor bedroom and put on a faded robe and well-worn bedroom slippers. They were big slippers, as they had to be to fit the president's very large feet.

Lincoln spent some time reading in the White House library, then went to his office to write several notes. One of these was to a man who had urged him to be on guard against assassins. Lincoln replied that he would "use due precaution," though he never really did.[4]

At 8:00 that morning, Lincoln joined his family for breakfast in a small dining room. The president was happy that his eldest son, Captain Robert Lincoln, was on leave from the army and could join his parents for the meal.[5]

Robert entered the room carrying a small portrait of General Robert E. Lee, commander of the Confederate armies. Lincoln gazed thoughtfully at the picture of the man who had been his opponent for so long. At last, he said, "It is a good face. It is the face of a noble, noble, brave man. I am glad the war is over at last."[6]

Later, Lincoln attended a meeting with his Cabinet. General Grant joined them. It was the first time he had been able to leave the battlefront to attend such a conference. Lincoln talked about rebuilding the country in the days ahead. Many hotheads in Congress wanted revenge upon the conquered South. But Lincoln said, "I hope there will be no persecution, no bloody work . . . Enough lives have been sacrificed."[7]

Some leaders of the Confederacy were planning to flee the country, afraid of Northern vengeance. Lincoln was in favor of letting them escape. He said, "When you have an elephant by the hind leg, and he's trying to run away, it's best to let him run."[8]

During a pause in business, General Grant told the president that he and his wife would not be able to go to Ford's Theatre with the Lincolns that night. The general said he was sorry, but his wife wanted to catch an afternoon train leaving Washington.

It is true that the Grants wanted to depart the city that day. But it also seems likely that Julia Grant did not wish to spend the evening with Mary Todd Lincoln. Not long before, the two women had shared a carriage when they visited a battle zone in Virginia. Mrs. Lincoln, exhausted and tense, suffered one of her "nervous attacks," becoming hysterical in Mrs. Grant's presence.[9] The general's wife had seen more

Lincoln's eldest son, Robert, was an officer in the Union Army. He was home on leave at the time of President Lincoln's assassination. He is shown here at an earlier age.

than enough of the excitable "hell cat," Mary Todd Lincoln.

The Grants' refusal of the theater invitation was one of those small acts that may have changed history. If the Grants had gone with Lincoln, everything about that fateful evening and its aftereffects might have been different.

Nancy Bushrod Calls on the President

About the time Lincoln was finishing his Cabinet meeting, an African-American woman arrived at the White House gate. She had walked five miles and was faint with hunger.

A guard stopped her and asked jokingly if she "had business with the president."

"Before God, yes!" she answered in a desperate tone.

"Let her pass," said the guard. Then he called to another sentry, "They'll stop her farther on."

The woman reached the main entrance, where she was again halted by sentries. Suddenly, the woman ducked under the guard's arm and ran to a door in the front hallway, begging to see President Lincoln.

The guard held her back, saying, "Madam, the president is busy. He cannot see you."

But her cries and the noise of the disturbance had carried inside. Abraham Lincoln himself appeared at the door, smiling and speaking softly. "There is time for all who need me. Let the good woman come in."

She introduced herself as Nancy Bushrod. She and her husband Tom had been slaves on the Harwood Plantation near Richmond until freed by the Emancipation Proclamation. Tom, like thousands of other freed slaves, joined the army to fight for the Union. He left Nancy with a baby girl and twin boys.

At first, money came from him the first of every month. Then the government fell behind in its payments and the money stopped. She had searched for work all over Washington but found nothing. The family ran out of food. The children were now hungry, and Mrs. Bushrod was desperate. Could Lincoln help her get Tom's pay?

"Come this time tomorrow, and the papers will be signed and ready for you," said Lincoln.

Nancy Bushrod was so moved that she could not speak. Tears were running down her cheeks. Lincoln started to leave, then turned back to her. He said, "Perhaps you'll see many a day when all the food in the house is a single loaf of bread. Even so, give every child a slice and send your children off to school."

With that, the president bowed to her, "Like I was a natural born lady," Nancy Bushrod said later.[10]

This was not the only occasion that day when Lincoln took time for an act of kindness. In the afternoon, Lincoln was preparing to leave for a carriage ride with his wife. A soldier who had lost an arm in battle was visiting the lower floor of the White House.

Lincoln happened to overhear him say, "I would almost give my other hand if I could shake that of Abraham Lincoln."

"You shall do that and it shall cost you nothing, my boy!" Lincoln exclaimed, approaching and grasping the young man's hand. He delayed another moment, asking the soldier about himself and praising his brave sacrifice.[11]

The Day's Final Duties

The president and Mrs. Lincoln took an afternoon ride in an open carriage. It was a beautiful day, and Mrs. Lincoln later said she "never saw him so cheerful."[12]

After the ride, the Lincolns had a rather hurried supper so the president could make his usual call at the War Department before going to the theater. This time, Lincoln actually had a bodyguard with him, a young man named William Crook. As they walked, they passed some drunken men who, like most of Washington, were celebrating the end of the war. But these fellows looked dangerous. For a moment, Lincoln seemed troubled.

He said, "I believe there are men who want to take my life." In a quiet tone, as though speaking to himself alone, he added, "And I have no doubt they will do it."

William Crook was startled. "Why do you think so, Mr. President?"

"Other men have been assassinated," Lincoln replied, still deep in thought.

"I hope you are mistaken, Mr. President."

"I know no one could do it and escape alive. But if it is to be done, it is impossible to prevent it."[13]

Crook was disturbed by the conversation. Later, he offered to stay on duty and guard the Lincolns at the theater. "No, Crook," Lincoln said kindly but firmly. "You have already had a long day's work. Go home to sleep and rest."[14]

At the War Department, Lincoln checked some telegrams and talked briefly with Secretary of War Stanton. Again, Stanton warned Lincoln against attending the theater, reminding the president that the city was full of dangerous characters. At least, Stanton insisted, have a good bodyguard.

During this visit, one of the telegraphers heard Lincoln say he did not really want to attend the play that night. But his presence had already been announced. "The public expects it," he said. "I cannot disappoint them."[15]

Back at the White House, Lincoln finished some last details. Mrs. Lincoln, fashionably dressed for an evening out, entered his office. "Well, Mr. Lincoln," she asked, "Are you going with me to the theater or not?"

Now, at the last moment, Lincoln hesitated. Then he said, "I suppose I have to go."

He found his hat and coat, then went to the door of Robert Lincoln's bedroom. "We are going to the theater, Bob. Don't you want to go?"

Young Robert Lincoln had just returned from the war front. He had not slept in a bed for two weeks. All he wanted to do was stay home and go to sleep early.

"Do what you most like, my boy," said Lincoln. The father and son then said good night.[16]

A few minutes later, President and Mrs. Lincoln entered the carriage that would take them on their last ride together.

THE NIGHT OF APRIL 14, 1865

The president's carriage paused just two blocks from the White House, at the home of Senator Ira Harris of New York. There, the Lincolns were joined by their guests of the evening, Clara Harris, the daughter of Senator Harris, and her fiancé, Major Henry Rathbone. Mary Todd Lincoln had invited the young couple after the Grants refused her invitation to the theater.

Major Rathbone had a fine record as a soldier in the war that had just ended. Lincoln was probably glad that Rathbone had joined them. Only an hour earlier, Secretary of War Stanton had again urged Lincoln to be accompanied by a protector if he went to the theater. The brave major fit the role of bodyguard, although he went simply as a guest.

The four people in the carriage were in a happy mood. A gray shadow of mist from the Potomac River was creeping through the streets of Washington. But it did not dampen the spirits of people celebrating on Pennsylvania Avenue. A victory parade was in progress. Flaming torches had been stuck into barrels to attract attention to Ford's Theatre. Barkers shouted at the parade marchers, struggling to be heard above the trumpets and drums. "This way to Ford's!"[1]

The presidential party arrived so late at the playhouse that the first act of *Our American Cousin* was well under way. When going to the theater, Abraham Lincoln usually tried to enter unnoticed. He did not want his arrival to distract the audience. But his tall figure was easy to recognize.

The party moved to the presidential box and closed the door behind them, but could not lock it. Lincoln found his usual rocking chair inside the box, and Mary took a straight chair beside him. On the opposite side, Clara Harris chose a chair next to a small sofa where Major Rathbone sat. Lincoln was near the door, Major Rathbone farther away.

Outside in the hallway a single guard had been stationed. This was John Parker, a patrolman who worked for the Metropolitan Police of Washington. Parker had a shabby history as a policeman. He had been charged with drunkenness, rudeness, and being asleep on duty. His behavior that night would add to his bad record. The Lincolns were hardly in their seats before Parker left his post to sit in the gallery and enjoy the comedy. Before long, he left the theater entirely to go next door with a friend for drinks. Lincoln was left completely unguarded.

During the next two hours, the auditorium was filled with happy laughter. Because of the draperies on the presidential box, only a few people in the audience could see inside, and even they could not see much.

Major Henry Rathbone, an outstanding soldier, was at Ford's Theatre as a guest of the Lincolns when the assassination took place.

Clearly, however, the Lincolns were having a good time and so were their guests. At times, though, Lincoln himself seemed to be lost in thought. He leaned forward against the railing, resting his chin on his hands, gazing at the audience.[2]

The Fatal Attack

Meanwhile, John Wilkes Booth had finished meeting with his conspirators at the Herndon Hotel. He had entered and left the theater several times. People who saw him later said he appeared nervous, restless, and excited. He talked to his old friend, the stagehand Edward Spangler, about having someone keep his horse ready behind the theater later. Spangler could not do it himself because he was working backstage. But a boy nicknamed Johnny Peanut did odd jobs at Ford's. Johnny Peanut would have the horse ready.

Soon after the start of the third act of the play, Booth silently climbed the stairs to the dress circle, then moved behind the seats to the nearby hallway. He barred the door behind him with a piece of a broken music stand. From under his coat, he drew a single-shot derringer pistol and a long, carefully sharpened knife.

The open doorway to the president's box was only a few steps ahead. He could see Major Rathbone quietly intent on the performance, unaware of any danger.

The Lincolns were sitting close together, holding hands. Mrs. Lincoln had whispered to her husband, "What will Miss Harris think of my hanging onto you so?"

Lincoln had already noticed that Miss Harris's hand was being held by the major. With a kind and affectionate smile, he replied, "She won't think anything about it."[3]

The action on the stage was spirited. This scene had one of the play's loudest laughs. Booth, who knew the comedy well, seemed to be counting on the laughter to cover the noise of a pistol shot.

Some of the broad humor of *Our American Cousin* came from the actors saying long, ridiculous-sounding words. Such a word was about to be uttered.

One of the actresses made a haughty exit, fuming that the "American cousin" did not know the manners of good society.

The actor playing the cousin replied, "I guess I know enough to turn you inside out, old gal—you sockdologizing old man trap!"[4]

The audience, as always, roared at the preposterous word, "sockdologizing."

Booth stepped behind Lincoln. Holding the weapon close to the back of the president's head, he pulled the trigger.

Major Rathbone, startled by the shot, looked around and saw Booth through a haze of gun smoke. He sprang forward to seize Booth as the actor dropped the gun and drew his knife. Booth slashed with the blade, opening a long wound in the major's arm. As Rathbone pulled back from the knife, Booth shouted something, perhaps the Latin motto of the state of Virginia, *"Sic semper tyrannis"* ("Thus always to

SOURCE DOCUMENT

WHEN THE SECOND SCENE OF THE THIRD ACT WAS BEING PERFORMED . . . I HEARD THE DISCHARGE OF A PISTOL BEHIND ME, AND, LOOKING ROUND, SAW THROUGH THE SMOKE A MAN BETWEEN THE DOOR AND THE PRESIDENT. . . . AT THE SAME TIME I HEARD THE MAN SHOUT SOME WORD, WHICH I THOUGHT WAS "FREEDOM!" I INSTANTLY SPRANG TOWARD HIM AND SEIZED HIM. HE . . . MADE A VIOLENT THRUST AT MY BREAST WITH A LARGE KNIFE. I PARRIED THE BLOW BY STRIKING IT UP, AND RECEIVED A WOUND SEVERAL INCHES DEEP IN MY LEFT ARM. . . . THE MAN RUSHED TO THE FRONT OF THE BOX, AND I ENDEAVORED TO SEIZE HIM AGAIN, BUT ONLY CAUGHT HIS CLOTHES AS HE WAS LEAPING OVER THE RAILING OF THE BOX.[5]

This is an excerpt from Major Henry Rathbone's account of what happened when John Wilkes Booth shot Lincoln at Ford's Theatre.

tyrants").[6] Then he vaulted over the railing and dropped to the stage.

One of Booth's spurs was caught in the cloth of a flag decorating the box. This threw Booth off balance, and he broke his leg when he landed. The injury did not stop him as he fled across the stage and escaped to an alley. He had completed his murderous work.

Atzerodt's Failed Mission

Elsewhere in the capital city that night, another conspirator was far less successful than Booth. George Atzerodt had been given the job of assassinating Vice President Andrew Johnson. He protested that Johnson was said to be a dangerous opponent, a tough fighter. Besides, Atzerodt had agreed to help commit a kidnapping, not a murder.

Booth had called Atzerodt a coward and insisted that the frightened man carry out his orders. Atzerodt, he said, must attack Andrew Johnson.

Atzerodt, completely disheartened, simply wandered around the city that night, unable to act. At last, he simply gave up. He threw away a knife he was carrying and pawned for ten dollars a pistol Booth had given him. Finally, Atzerodt found a bed and went to sleep. Vice President Johnson was safe.

The Attack on Seward

That same night, Secretary of State William Seward lay ill in an upstairs bedroom of a spacious house near the Capitol Building. A week before, he had been riding in a carriage when the horse bolted. Seward was thrown to the street, suffering a broken arm, a concussion, and a jaw so badly shattered that it had to be clamped with a steel brace. His condition was still very serious.

A little after 10:00 P.M., about the time Booth was entering the presidential box at Ford's, there was a knock at the door of the Seward residence.

The house was closed for the night. The injured man lay half asleep upstairs, and all the gaslights had been turned low. William Bell, a former slave who now worked for the Sewards, answered the door. A tall man with a hat pulled down over one eye stood there holding a small package.

"I have medicine from Doctor Verdi . . ." he said. "It has to be delivered personally."[7]

Bell told the caller that Seward could not be disturbed, but the man simply brushed past the servant and moved toward the stairs. He seemed so sure of himself that Bell believed the story about the medicine. Bell would show Lewis Paine, posing as a deliveryman, to Seward's bedroom.

Frederick Seward, the secretary's son, heard heavy footsteps on the stairs. When he tried to block the way, the stranger pulled out a pistol and, using it as a club, beat Frederick almost senseless. Fanny Seward, on duty in her father's bedroom, rushed to see what was causing the commotion outside. Paine pushed past her, brandishing a knife.

He hurled himself at the half-conscious man in the bed. He stabbed again and again, not realizing that most of his thrusts only slashed the large nightgown Seward wore, his blade possibly turned aside by the invalid's steel neck brace. Seward, with three stab wounds and his nightgown in ribbons, rolled from the bed. The narrowness of the space between the bed and the wall protected him, and although horribly hurt, Seward survived.

Seward's nurse George Robinson and Seward's other son, Augustus, seized Paine. The attacker gave Augustus seven knife wounds before Paine broke away and fled downstairs shouting, "I'm mad! I'm mad!"[8]

In the first-floor hall, Paine met a messenger from the State Department who had heard the noise and rushed to help. The messenger was nearly killed with a single knife thrust before Paine fled into the night.

William Bell, in an act of great bravery, followed Paine outside and chased him down the street, shouting, "Murder!" But he was unable to find help and gave up when Paine mounted a horse.[9]

Bell did not notice another man on a horse, watching in the shadows. It was David Herold, the conspirator Booth had assigned to guide Paine. At this point, Herold decided that Paine's job was finished. He rode off in another direction.

Alarm in Washington

There was confusion and fear at the Seward house. Doctors, soldiers, and government officials were arriving. Word came that the president had been shot and might be near death. The Seward household, and soon all of Washington, was near panic. There were

Lewis Paine, on his way upstairs to kill Secretary of State William Seward, met Frederick Seward on the stairs. He used his pistol as a club. This engraving appeared in Harper's *magazine soon after the attack took place.*

wild rumors about a Confederate attack. A story spread that rebel prisoners had escaped from prison and were burning the city. Soon police officers and soldiers were patrolling the streets, not knowing what to expect. Every available man was put on duty.

"Burn Ford's Theatre!"

Angry and frightened citizens were forming mobs. "Burn Ford's Theatre!" someone shouted. Others, about two thousand people, marched on the Old Capital Prison, crying out that it should be burned with the prisoners of war inside it. Only the police and soldiers stopped this from happening.[10]

It was one of the most terrible nights in the history of the nation's capital, a night that the people of Washington, D.C., would never forget.

Meanwhile, in a house across the street from the theater, Abraham Lincoln hovered between life and death.

"NOW HE BELONGS TO THE AGES"

The cry, "The president is shot!" had caused alarm and terrible confusion inside Ford's Theatre. People milled about, jamming the aisles. Some stood on seats, trying to see what had happened.

Laura Keene, the star of *Our American Cousin*, had been waiting just offstage, ready to enter, when the shot was fired. A moment later, Booth raced past her so close that his hand actually brushed her arm. He had just crossed the stage and was running toward the door to an alley where a horse awaited him. Now the actress stepped to the footlights and spoke to the audience, pleading for calm. Her words and cool manner helped prevent panic.

Many of the spectators had recognized John Wilkes Booth when he leaped to the stage. Soon his name was being shouted in the auditorium, along with cries of "Shoot him!" and "Kill him!" and "Lynch him!"[1]

Dr. Charles Leale, a young army surgeon in the audience, was one of the first to reach the wounded president.

"Oh, Doctor, is he dead?" Mary Lincoln asked. "Can he recover?"[2] Mrs. Lincoln was numb with shock. Soon she would begin to weep without control.

Dr. Charles Taft arrived a moment later and began to help Leale, who was doing what he could for the president. The doctors quickly found a single, massive wound to Lincoln's skull. They thought his head should be slightly raised, so Laura Keene held Lincoln's head in her lap, his blood staining her yellow dress.

Throughout the theater, there was noise and confusion. The doctors examining Lincoln agreed he should be taken to the nearest house. The White House was too far away, seven blocks over rough streets. Lincoln's hold on life was too frail to risk a bumpy journey in a wagon or carriage.

A crowd eager for news had gathered outside the presidential box. An army officer had to threaten them with his sword before they would make way so Lincoln could be moved down the stairs.

In the Peterson House

The president was carried across the street to a brick house owned by William Peterson and placed on a bed in a small room at the rear. In the past, Lincoln had sometimes complained that many beds were too short for him. This was also true in the Peterson house. The president's tall form had to be placed diagonally on the bed. The mattress was stuffed with corn husks, just like the beds Lincoln had slept on as a boy.

THE PRESIDENT HAD BEEN CARRIED ACROSS THE STREET FROM THE THEATRE TO THE HOUSE OF A MR. PETERSON. WE ENTERED BY ASCENDING A FLIGHT OF STEPS ABOVE THE BASEMENT AND PASSING THROUGH A LONG HALL TO THE REAR, WHERE THE PRESIDENT LAY, EXTENDED ON A BED, BREATHING HEAVILY. . . .

THE GIANT SUFFERER LAY EXTENDED DIAGONALLY ACROSS THE BED, WHICH WAS NOT LONG ENOUGH FOR HIM. HE HAD BEEN STRIPPED OF HIS CLOTHES. HIS LARGE ARMS, WHICH WERE OCCASIONALLY EXPOSED, WERE OF A SIZE WHICH ONE WOULD SCARCE HAVE EXPECTED FROM HIS SPARE APPEARANCE. HIS SLOW, FULL RESPIRATION LIFTED THE CLOTHES WITH EACH BREATH HE TOOK. HIS FEATURES WERE CALM AND STRIKING. I HAD NEVER SEEN THEM APPEAR TO BETTER ADVANTAGE THAN FOR THE FIRST HOUR, PERHAPS, THAT I WAS THERE.[3]

Gideon Welles was secretary of the Navy under President Lincoln. This is an excerpt from his account of what happened the night of Lincoln's assassination.

Mary Todd Lincoln, delayed by the excited, pushing crowd outside the theater, arrived and rushed to her husband's side, sobbing. Major Rathbone had come with Mrs. Lincoln but was too weak from loss of blood to get past the hallway. He soon fainted, and Clara Harris saved his life by binding his arm tightly with her handkerchief, stopping the flow of blood from the knife wound Booth had given him.

Dr. Charles Leale, Army Surgeon

Almost from the beginning, the doctors were fairly sure that Lincoln could not recover. The bullet had done too much damage to his brain. Five physicians did their best, yet all knew it was a losing battle. Still, Lincoln was an unusually strong man. He had lived a rugged life of hard work and exercise. No one could be sure of what might happen as the minutes and then the hours went by.

A hero of the night was the twenty-three-year-old surgeon, Dr. Charles Leale. The young doctor had always felt a deep admiration for Abraham Lincoln. He had gone to the theater that night not just to see a play, but to catch a glimpse of the president who had saved the American nation.

In the Peterson house, he worked unceasingly to ease Lincoln's suffering, never giving up hope for a miracle. When there was little of medical value he could do, he simply held Lincoln's hand, "To let him know in his blindness, if possible, that he was in touch with humanity and had a friend."[4]

Stanton Takes Command

Cabinet members and other officials arrived at the house. Vice President Johnson looked in, then went away under heavy protection in case there were other assassins in the city. He was told that Lincoln might not survive, and that he should be ready to take the oath of office as president soon.

Secretary of War Edwin Stanton took charge of the Peterson house, and actually of the whole government that night. For several hours, the small brick building became the capital and control center of the United States, with Edwin Stanton in complete command. Working in a room near the one where the president lay, Stanton issued swift, positive orders.

First, he had the house surrounded by armed soldiers in case the city was truly under attack by rebels. There was no attack, of course, and no rebellion in Washington. But for many hours, Stanton was unsure of what was happening.

By telegraph, Stanton ordered General Grant to return at once from Philadelphia, where the Grants were staying on their way to New Jersey. He also summoned detectives from New York City to begin an investigation of the attack on the president.

Stanton felt it was important to give the press his version of what was happening. He knew there would be endless rumors and mistaken reports, so he tried to issue an official story. That was difficult when he himself was in the dark.

Lincoln's final hours were spent in the Peterson house, now a museum. Today, the rooms seem cramped and dim, but in the 1860s, it was considered "one of the best houses of its class" in Washington.

To add to the confusion, the commercial telegraph lines out of Washington suddenly stopped working. To Stanton, this seemed like more evidence of rebellion and sabotage. Actually, the cause was simply a mechanical failure and normal service was quickly restored.

Quite early, Stanton began hearing the name John Wilkes Booth. Countless people in Ford's Theatre had identified the actor as the assassin. Some of the witnesses arrived at the Peterson house and gave statements. Stanton heard much of what they said, for he sat in the same room issuing orders and summoning officials.

A shorthand reporter took down the words of the witnesses. This was no easy job because of the noise and confusion around them. In the next room, separated only by a thin folding door, Mary Todd Lincoln was almost wild with grief, weeping loudly and begging her husband not to die and leave her. She insisted frantically that she had not really wanted to go to the theater that night. Once, she fainted. Twice, she had to be led away from Lincoln's bedside when her cries became too disturbing. Finally, Stanton ordered her kept out of the room where the president lay. Robert Lincoln arrived to keep watch near his father.

A Lone Assassin?

Army officers and government officials kept coming and going. The tramp of soldiers' boots and the calls of sentries sounded in the street outside. The steel-shod hooves of horses rang on the cobblestoned streets as cavalry rode past on the way to defend the city against any surprise invasion.

Meanwhile, Edwin Stanton kept working steadily and rapidly. It did not take him long to find out who had actually pulled the trigger of the pistol in Ford's Theatre. All of Washington had quickly heard Booth identified by eyewitnesses to the crime. Yet for the first hour or so, Stanton was cautious about accusing Booth. Then, in the second report he sent to the press, he wrote, "Investigation strongly indicates J. Wilkes Booth as the assassin."[5]

Stanton simply did not want to accept that one man, an actor, could have carried out such a great crime by himself. It seemed easier to believe that the assassination was a vast plot designed by the Confederacy. Could Booth have hatched and carried out the whole scheme by himself?

It is now generally believed that he did. The evidence has been carefully sifted and resifted. Yet the same questions that bothered Edwin Stanton have worried other investigators ever since. Almost all those who have carefully studied the assassination believe that Booth acted alone with some help from a few followers. Recently, several scholars have tried to link Booth to a larger plot by the Confederate Secret Service. So far, there has been little evidence to support this. For now, at least, the view that Booth was the independent ringleader of a very small band of plotters is considered true.

Booth Flees to the South

While Lincoln lay struggling against death in the Peterson house, John Wilkes Booth was riding through the night into Maryland.

Except for the injury to his leg, his escape had gone exactly as he had planned it. His horse had been waiting for him outside the alley door of the theater. After kicking the boy who held his horse's reins, Booth rode swiftly to Pennsylvania Avenue, Washington's main thoroughfare. Soon he turned a corner and plunged into a dark, dingy neighborhood where he was not likely to be recognized.

Booth crossed the carelessly guarded Navy Bridge into Maryland, where he met David Herold, the young conspirator who had earlier led assassin Lewis Paine to the Seward house. The two rode together toward Surrattsville.

They had much to tell each other. Booth believed that Lincoln had died instantly. He was, of course, mistaken. Herold wrongly thought Lewis Paine had succeeded in killing Secretary of State Seward.

Booth's greatest worry now was his injured leg. He could not tell if it was sprained or broken but knew he must soon find a doctor.

Dr. Mudd's Strange Patient

At the tavern in Surrattsville, Booth was given directions to the farm of Dr. Samuel Mudd. Booth had met the doctor before, a casual meeting at a church. Once, the doctor had helped arrange for Booth to buy a horse. But they knew each other only slightly. Mudd was a prominent man in the neighborhood, so Booth had quite a bit of information about him. The doctor was a Southern sympathizer, perhaps even a Confederate patriot. Before the Emancipation Proclamation, he had used slaves to work his large farm. Once, when a slave refused to obey an order, Mudd had simply shot him in the leg. Still, Booth did not trust the doctor. So he put on a theatrical disguise he was carrying, the whiskers of an old man.[6]

At about 4:00 A.M., Booth and Herold rode up to Mudd's dark farmhouse. Booth hoped that within an hour the doctor could fix his leg well enough to allow riding. He and Herold could then go on to Virginia, where Booth thought they would be safe and welcome as heroes of the South.

Booth Misjudges the South

Booth was completely wrong about the feelings of Virginians. Most of them, when they learned about the assassination, were horrified. Murder was not their way of fighting a war. They found political assassination cowardly and repulsive. The assassination of the president was a terrible blow to the whole country, but the ones who would suffer most were Southerners.

Mary Chesnut, a writer and wife of a prominent Southerner, wrote in her diary in South Carolina, "Lincoln, old Abe Lincoln has been killed . . . Why? . . .

I know this foul murder will bring upon us worse miseries."[7] Many Southerners realized that the kind and forgiving Abraham Lincoln was the best man for the South to deal with in defeat.

While surrendering to Union General William T. Sherman, Confederate General Joseph E. Johnston learned of the assassination. He called it "the greatest possible calamity to the South."[8]

John Wilkes Booth, thinking of himself as a great hero, completely failed to see the harm he had done to people he hoped to rescue.

Soon, an army would be hunting him. Besides soldiers and police, thousands of ordinary people would be on the watch for Booth. In a few days, Secretary of War Stanton would advertise a reward of twenty-five thousand dollars for the assassin. This was a fortune at the time, by far the largest amount that had ever been offered for the capture of a criminal in the United States.

The Death of the President

Not long after 7:00 A.M. on April 15, 1865, Abraham Lincoln, his body worn out from the struggle, took his last breath. Robert Lincoln was at his bedside. Mary Todd Lincoln, helped in from the next room, was so overcome by grief that she had to be led away, shaking and sobbing.

There was silence in the small bedroom of the Peterson house. Morning light gleamed through the

Posters offering rewards for the capture of the fugitives were quickly circulated through all the states near Washington, D.C. The rewards were by far the largest that had ever been offered in the United States.

window as Lincoln's friends stood with bowed heads. They felt shattered by the loss of the president. Their world had suddenly become a very different and less kind place. It was Edwin Stanton who then spoke the words that would soon be repeated throughout the country and later known all over the world: "Now he belongs to the ages."[9]

AFTERMATH: GRIEF AND REVENGE

The news of Lincoln's death added to the fear and panic in Washington, D.C. The city seethed with rumors. Some said Andrew Johnson and all the Cabinet had been murdered. Other people claimed rebels would soon set the whole city ablaze. It was said that General Grant had been killed on board his train, that the government had been destroyed, and that no one remained in charge. None of this was true, but most people feared the worst.

Churchbells throughout Washington began to toll round the clock to mourn Lincoln. Cannons in all parts of the city were fired in salute to the lost leader. The big guns roared every half hour, day and night. The ringing and roaring added terrible stress to the frayed nerves of the people.

Although Andrew Johnson was now president, for the time being, Secretary of War Edwin Stanton remained in charge. He saw that two matters had to be taken care of before America could begin to return to normal: Those guilty of Lincoln's death had to be

Vice President Andrew Johnson of Tennessee had also been marked for assassination but was not actually attacked. He became the seventeenth president of the United States.

caught and punished, and at the same time, the nation's mourning for the slain president had to be arranged.

There would be memorial services for Lincoln in Washington on April 19, 1865. But his actual funeral was to take place in Springfield, Illinois, at the beginning of May.

Stanton Rounds up Suspects

Stanton and other leaders were determined to have the assassins arrested, tried, and executed before the mourning for Lincoln was over. So a massive manhunt was launched.

John Wilkes Booth had left behind so much evidence of the conspiracy that there was little mystery about it. Most of the plotters were quickly found.

Lewis Paine was arrested when he went to the Surratt house pretending to be a workman. Witnesses quickly identified him as the man who had attacked Seward. Dr. Mudd was seized at his Maryland farm. He was arrested after a boot belonging to Booth was found in his house. The actor had left the useless boot behind after Mudd bandaged his leg. Other suspects, including some who were innocent, were soon in the hands of the police.

Stanton ordered the arrest of everyone who had even a distant connection with the assassination. Soon, Washington's jails bulged with suspects and witnesses, and their friends and relatives. Laura Keene and other actors from *Our American Cousin* found themselves imprisoned. Countless people suffered harsh questioning. Many were terrorized, mistreated, and held without being charged.[1]

Acting only on suspicion, Stanton announced that the killing of Lincoln had been planned in Canada by Confederate fugitives, including Mary Surratt's son, John. The evil plan had then been approved in Richmond, Virginia, by a group of Southern leaders. No evidence of this was offered. But it inflamed the hatred of a nation mourning its slain president.

The Death of John Wilkes Booth

For several days, John Wilkes Booth and David Herold remained at large. They had left Dr. Mudd's house as soon as Booth was able to ride. Hiding in swamps and woods, fearful and in pain, the murderer was learning that every person was now his enemy. Booth and Herold managed to cross into Virginia, where Booth found himself a hunted and hated fugitive, not a hero.

At last, they took refuge in a tobacco barn where they were soon surrounded. David Herold, in despair, quickly surrendered. John Wilkes Booth, however, was armed and determined to resist.

The barn was set afire. Booth might have died in the flames, but a trooper shot through a gap between two boards of the barn wall. Booth was hit in the back. Mortally wounded, he was dragged from the blazing building. Looking at his own hands, he said, "Useless! Useless!" and died.[2]

David Herold was taken prisoner and returned to Washington in chains for trial.

The Secret Burial of Booth

On Booth's body were found two pistols, a knife, a compass, a pipe, and a small diary bound in leather.[3] The diary contained information that might have been valuable at the upcoming trial of the conspirators. However, the authorities kept it from being used as evidence. What Booth had written showed that the assassination was not a grand plot hatched by the Confederacy. It also revealed that most of the conspirators thought they were joining a scheme to commit kidnapping, not murder. These were not welcome facts to the officials in Washington.

Stanton immediately ordered Booth's body to be buried in secret. Historian Margaret Leech has described the scene:

> A shallow hole was scraped in the floor of a ground-floor storage room in the old Penitentiary . . . At midnight, by the light of a single lantern flickering over gun boxes and packing cases, Booth's body was dropped in the hole . . . The storage room was locked, and the key delivered to Mr. Stanton. The few men who knew of the burial place were sworn to secrecy.[4]

Stanton seemed to be afraid that Confederates would make a shrine of Booth's grave. Apparently, he did not understand the feelings of Southerners any better than Booth himself had. No one respected or honored a man who fought by stealth and murder. Booth was considered a coward, not a hero.

Because of the swift and secret burial, rumors spread that the body was not really Booth's. Some people said Booth had actually escaped. Years later, the body was moved from the prison at the request of the Booth family. At that time, it was positively identified as the assassin's.

The Trial of the Plotters

The other conspirators were treated with brutality, even tortured. The public, outraged by Lincoln's death, did not protest the cruelty. The accused prisoners were looked upon as savage animals.

Eight prisoners were charged with conspiring with Jefferson Davis and other Confederate government officials to murder Lincoln, Grant, Seward, and Johnson. This was the same accusation Stanton had made earlier. Neither then nor later was there a scrap of proof to connect the South with the crime.

The trial was illegal by any civilized standards. The prisoners were brought into court covered with the heavy hoods they were forced to wear in their cells. Behind the canvas, it was almost impossible to speak, eat, or even breathe. The hoods were supposed to prevent the prisoners from escaping by keeping them blind. Actually, they seemed to have been intended to inflict punishment. When the hoods were taken off in court, the prisoners were blinded by the light. They looked wild and dangerous.

John Wilkes Booth's diary, which might have cleared some of the prisoners, was kept out of evidence.

Also, the prisoners were tried before a military court, making it easier to convict them on doubtful evidence.

Lewis Paine and George Atzerodt were easily convicted and sentenced to death. David Herold quickly suffered the same fate.

Mary Surratt was a different case. The evidence against her was flimsy and unclear. Acquaintances remembered her as sweet and motherly. In court, the clank of chains beneath her long skirt aroused pity. The case against her seemed to come down to the fact that plotting was done in her boardinghouse, so she *must* have known about it. Also, her son John was a Confederate messenger, now a fugitive in Canada. Legally, none of this should have mattered, yet she seemed so deeply involved with the plot that it was hard to consider her innocent.

For a military court to sentence a woman to death was shocking to many people—she would be the first woman ever executed by the United States government. Nevertheless, Mary Surratt was condemned to hang with the three men.

The conspirators sentenced to death were hanged in a courtyard of the Old Capital Prison on a hot July day in 1865. Until the last moment, friends and sympathizers of Mary Surratt believed President Johnson would save her from death, but this did not happen. It is reported that one guard was gentlemanly enough to hold an umbrella over her head as she stood on the gallows.

The convicted conspirators were executed by hanging on July 7, 1865. Many people expected Mary Surratt to escape death at the last moment, but President Andrew Johnson refused to commute her sentence.

Prison Sentences

Four others, Dr. Mudd, Edward Spangler, Samuel Arnold, and Michael O'Laughlin, were each given a prison sentence that was nearly equivalent to a death sentence. They would serve their time on the hot and barren Dry Tortugas islands off the coast of Florida. Prisoners were not likely to live long there.

Dr. Mudd had actually done nothing but treat an injured stranger in the middle of the night, certainly no crime. It was never shown that he knew anything about the assassination when he attended Booth. Still, Mudd appeared guilty to the court. He was devoted to slavery and the Confederacy and his hatred of African Americans was deep. When he did learn about the assassination of Lincoln, he delayed reporting his late-night patient. Despite Booth's false whiskers, it seems likely that Mudd recognized him.

While imprisoned in dreadful conditions in Dry Tortugas, Mudd did heroic work during a yellow fever outbreak. President Johnson pardoned him in 1869.

Edward Spangler, the stagehand at Ford's Theatre, was sentenced to six years for helping Booth escape. There was no evidence that he did so. But Spangler was a friend and admirer of Booth, and he worked at Ford's. That was enough to convict him. He, too, was later pardoned.

Less innocent was Samuel Arnold, Booth's old friend from school, who had been persuaded to help kidnap Lincoln. Later, he had withdrawn from the plot, but this did not save him from imprisonment. He was given a life sentence but, like Mudd and Spangler, was eventually pardoned.

Michael O'Laughlin, the other schoolmate of Booth, had also quit the kidnapping plot. Still, he was sent to the Dry Tortugas on a thin suspicion that he had planned to assassinate General Grant at a fireworks display. He died of yellow fever in prison.

A Grieving Nation

Never had America seen anything like the national mourning for Abraham Lincoln. In Philadelphia, the driver of a horse-drawn city bus halted to take the bells off the horses' harness. They, too, would be in mourning. An old woman in Cleveland, once a slave, worked to gather pine branches, then traveled to place them on Lincoln's casket. In New York, a banner rose over Broadway. It said, "The great person, the great man, is the miracle of history."[5]

There was a threatening tone in the great hymn to Lincoln. Leaders across the North, including preachers, editors, and politicians, vowed vengeance against the South for Lincoln's slaying. Some members of Congress would use Booth's crime as an excuse to inflict heavier punishments on the defeated Southern states.

Confederate General Robert E. Lee spoke of his sadness at the news and said he had "surrendered as much to [Lincoln's] goodness as to Grant's artillery."[6] Jefferson Davis, in hiding, expressed the same fear that the South, perhaps more than the North, had suffered a terrible blow.[7] He was right.

The Return to Springfield

The seven-car train bearing Lincoln's casket left Washington on April 21, 1865. Bound for Springfield, Illinois, it would follow much the same route Lincoln had taken to Washington a little more than four years earlier.

In Baltimore, where his life had been threatened, the train was greeted with reverence and deep sorrow. The city had changed, and Lincoln had helped change it.

The black-draped train rolled slowly on to New York, through Pennsylvania, across the Midwest.

In Illinois, throngs of mourners awaited it. Among them was a very old woman, Sally Bush Lincoln, Abraham Lincoln's stepmother. When news of his death had been brought to her prairie farmhouse, she had said, "I knowed when he went away, he'd never come back alive."[8]

At last, the train reached Springfield, Illinois. This was where he had first received threats of violent death. This was also where he first resolved that fear of violence would not keep him from doing what he thought was right, what he believed in.

On May 4, 1865, a great and solemn procession moved slowly from the Illinois State Capitol to the Oak Ridge Cemetery. There, Abraham Lincoln would be laid to rest. Thousands gathered on the green lawns to listen to the hymns, to hear eloquent praise of the

Cities across the country held funerals and memorial services for Abraham Lincoln. This one took place in New York, where the black-draped train paused on its way to Lincoln's hometown of Springfield, Illinois.

fallen leader, the poor boy who had risen to greatness, who had ended slavery and saved the Union.

No words better summed up his life and his faith than some of his own. They were read aloud that day, the closing lines of one of his greatest speeches, his Second Inaugural Address.

"With malice toward none; with charity for all; with firmness in the right, as God gives us to see the right, let us strive on to finish the work we are in . . . to do all which may achieve and cherish a just, and lasting peace, among ourselves, and with all nations."[9]

★ TIMELINE ★

1858—*August*: Debates between Abraham Lincoln and Stephen Douglas in Illinois show Lincoln to be a foe of slavery.

1858—*November*: Lincoln fails to be elected senator, but has become an important national figure.

1860—*May*: Republicans nominate Lincoln as their candidate for the presidency of the United States.

1860—*November 6*: Lincoln is elected president without winning a single Southern state.

1860—*December*: Lincoln receives first threats and hate mail from supporters of slavery; South Carolina withdraws from the Union.

1861—*February*: Threats and dangers mar Lincoln's train trip from Springfield, Illinois, to Washington, D.C.; He passes through Baltimore, Maryland, in secret.

1861—*March 4*: Lincoln is inaugurated as president.

1861—*April 12*: Rebel cannons open fire on Fort Sumter in the harbor of Charleston, South Carolina; The Civil War begins.

1861—*April 20*: Railroads are blocked between Baltimore and Washington, D.C.; Attack on the capital feared.

1861—*May*: Washington is fortified against possible attacks; Baltimore occupied by Union troops.

1862—*January*: Edwin Stanton becomes secretary of war and takes charge of protecting Lincoln.

1862—*April 16*: Slavery abolished by Congress in District of Columbia; Lincoln approves.

1862—*Summer and Fall*: The North and South struggle with much bloodshed but no clear results; Lincoln is discouraged.

1863—*January 1*: The Emancipation Proclamation frees many slaves; John Wilkes Booth and others who want to keep slavery are horrified.

1863—*July 1–4*: Union victories in battles at Gettysburg, Pennsylvania, and Vicksburg, Mississippi, are turning points in the Civil War.

1863—*November*: John Wilkes Booth plays for the first time in Ford's Theatre; Lincoln sees him in *The Marble Heart*.

1864—*January and February*: It seems probable that Booth is serving as a Confederate spy and smuggler.

1864—*Spring and Summer*: Union victories show that the North is winning the war; Booth begins plotting, hoping to kidnap Lincoln before the November election.

1864—*May*: President and Mrs. Lincoln are threatened by an unruly crowd outside Grover's Theatre.

1864—*November 8*: Lincoln is reelected president.

1865—*January and February*: Booth enlists his friends to aid in his plot against Lincoln.

1865—*March 7*: Lincoln is inaugurated as president.

1865—*March 17*: Conspirators wait in ambush to seize Lincoln at Soldiers' Home hospital; He does not appear.

1865—*April 3*: Richmond, Virginia, falls to Union armies.

1865—*April 6*: Secretary of State Seward is seriously injured in a carriage accident, an event that will shape part of Booth's assassination plans.

1865—*April 9*: General Robert E. Lee surrenders to General Ulysses S. Grant at Appomattox Court House.

1865—*April 11*: Lincoln makes a speech proposing limited voting rights for freed slaves; Booth and others resolve to kill him.

1865—*April 14*: Booth shoots Lincoln in Ford's Theatre; Lewis Paine attacks and seriously injures Secretary of State Seward and his son Frederick.

1865—*April 15*: Abraham Lincoln dies; Booth is a fugitive in Maryland; Andrew Johnson is sworn in as president of the United States.

1865—*April 19*: Funeral services for President Lincoln in Washington, D.C.

1865—*April 21*: Lincoln's funeral train leaves Washington, D.C.; It will travel sixteen hundred miles through the mourning nation to arrive in Springfield, Illinois, on May 2.

1865—*April 26*: Booth found and shot near Port Royal, Virginia.

1865—*April 30*: Booth buried secretly at midnight in an unmarked grave.

1865—*May 10–June 30*: Trial of the Lincoln conspirators.

1865—*July 7*: Execution of the convicted Lincoln conspirators.

★ CHAPTER NOTES ★

Chapter 1

1. Jim Bishop, *The Day Lincoln Was Shot* (New York: Harper & Row, 1955), p. 42.

2. Ibid., p. 135.

3. W. Emerson Reck, *A. Lincoln: His Last 24 Hours* (Columbia: University of South Carolina Press, 1994), p. 113.

Chapter 2

1. Henry J. Raymond, *The Life and Public Services of Abraham Lincoln* (New York: Derby & Miller, 1865), p. 779.

2. Ibid., p. 781.

3. W. Emerson Reck, *A. Lincoln: His Last 24 Hours* (Columbia: University of South Carolina Press, 1994), p. 14.

4. Carl Sandburg, *Abraham Lincoln* (New York: Harcourt Brace Jovanovich, Inc., 1974), p. 183.

5. Russell Freedman, *Lincoln: A Photobiography* (New York: Clarion Books, 1987), p. 59.

6. Ibid., p. 61.

7. Paul M. Angle, *A Lincoln Reader* (Newark, N.J.: Rutgers University Press, 1947), p. 57.

8. Freedman, p. 60.

9. Sandburg, p. 183.

10. Ibid., p. 184.

11. Raymond, p. 294.

12. Ibid.

13. Edward D. Neill, *Reminiscences of the Last Year of President Lincoln's Life* (St. Paul, Minn.: St. Paul Book and Stationery Co., 1887), n.p.

14. Margaret Leech, *Reveille in Washington* (Alexandria, Va.: Time-Life Books, Inc., 1980), p. 354.

15. Ibid., p. 56.

16. Sandburg, p. 184.

Chapter 3

1. Abraham Lincoln, *The Writings of Abraham Lincoln* (New York: Random House, 1940), p. 636.

2. Henry J. Raymond, *The Life and Public Services of Abraham Lincoln* (New York: Derby & Miller, 1865), p. 788.

3. Ward Hill Lamon, *The Life of Abraham Lincoln* (Boston: James R. Osgood & Co., 1872), p. 182.

4. Carl Sandburg, *Abraham Lincoln* (New York: Harcourt Brace Jovanovich, Inc., 1974), p. 198.

5. Lamon, p. 187.

6. Ibid., p. 192.

7. Raymond, p. 367.

8. Ibid.

9. Sandburg, p. 203.

10. Ibid., p. 207.

Chapter 4

1. Henry J. Raymond, *The Life and Public Services of Abraham Lincoln* (New York: Derby & Miller, 1865), p. 301.

2. Margaret Leech, *Reveille in Washington* (Alexandria, Va.: Time-Life Books, Inc., 1980), p. 60.

3. Carl Sandburg, *Abraham Lincoln* (New York: Harcourt Brace Jovanovich, Inc., 1974), p. 204.

4. Frederick Seward, *Reminiscences of a War-Time Statesman and Diplomat* (New York: G. P. Putnam's Sons, 1916), p. 87.

5. Ibid.

6. Raymond, p. 307.

7. Ibid., p. 308.

8. Ibid.

9. Ibid., p. 309.

10. Ward Hill Lamon, *The Life of Abraham Lincoln* (Boston: James R. Osgood & Co., 1872), p. 187.

11. Abraham Lincoln, *The Writings of Abraham Lincoln* (New York: Random House, 1940), p. 644.

12. Lamon, p. 189.

13. Ibid., p. 190.

14. Sandburg, p. 206.

15. Lamon, p. 191.

16. James D. Horan and Howard Sureggett, *The Pinkerton Story* (New York: Putnam, 1941), p. 87.

17. Ibid., p. 89.

18. Seward, p. 95.

Chapter 5

1. Carl Sandburg, *Abraham Lincoln* (New York: Harcourt Brace Jovanovich, Inc., 1974), p. 208.

2. Henry J. Raymond, *The Life and Public Services of Abraham Lincoln* (New York: Derby & Miller, 1865), p. 576.

3. Ward Hill Lamon, *The Life of Abraham Lincoln* (Boston: James R. Osgood & Co., 1872), p. 214.

4. Margaret Leech, *Reveille in Washington* (Alexandria, Va.: Time-Life Books, Inc., 1980), p. 4.

5. In Richard Hofstadter, ed., *Great Issues in American History: From the Revolution to the Civil War, 1765–1865* (New York: Vintage Books, 1958), pp. 396–397.

6. Abraham Lincoln, *The Writings of Abraham Lincoln* (New York: Random House, 1940), p. 657.

7. Leech, p. 93.

8. Raymond, p. 601.

Chapter 6

1. John Hay, *Diaries and Letters of John Hay* (New York: Dodd Mead and Co., 1939), p. 167.

2. O. H. Oldroyd, *The Assassination of Abraham Lincoln* (Washington, D.C.: O.H. Oldroyd, 1901), p. 42.

3. Asia Booth Clarke, *The Unlocked Book* (New York: J.B. Putnam's Sons, 1938), p. 38.

4. Ibid., p. 37.

5. Ibid., p. 39.

6. Ibid., p. 56.

7. Oldroyd, p. 60.

8. W. Emerson Reck, *A. Lincoln: His Last 24 Hours* (Columbia: University of South Carolina Press, 1994), p. 66.

9. Paul M. Angle, *A Lincoln Reader* (Newark, N.J.: Rutgers University Press, 1947), p. 160.

10. Henry J. Raymond, *The Life and Public Services of Abraham Lincoln* (New York: Derby & Miller, 1865), p. 609.

11. Reck, p. 66.

Chapter 7

1. W. Emerson Reck, *A. Lincoln: His Last 24 Hours* (Columbia: University of South Carolina Press, 1994), p. 66.

2. Ward Hill Lamon, *The Life of Abraham Lincoln* (Boston: James R. Osgood & Co., 1872), p. 18.

3. Ibid.

4. Reck, p. 69.

5. Ibid., p. 70.

6. William H. Crook, *Through Five Administrations* (New York: Harper Bros., 1910), p. 1.

7. Ben Purley Poore, *The Conspiracy Trial for the Murder of the President* (Boston: J. E. Tilton, 1865–1866), vol. 1, p. 19.

8. U.S. Congress, *Impeachment Investigation House Report*, no. 7., Washington, D.C., 1867, p. 783.

9. Ibid., p. 797.

10. John Y. Simon, ed., *The Personal Memoirs of Julia Dent Grant* (New York: G. P. Putnam's Sons, 1975), p. 155.

11. George J. Olszewski, *The Restoration of Ford's Theatre* (Washington, D.C.: National Park Service, 1963), p. 43.

12. John Lawrence, "An Unsung Song Prevented Panic When Lincoln Was Shot," American Press Association, 1912.

13. Ibid.

Chapter 8

1. Ward Hill Lamon, *The Life of Abraham Lincoln* (Boston: James R. Osgood & Co., 1872) p. 193.

2. Ibid., p. 194.

3. W. Emerson Reck, *A. Lincoln: His Last 24 Hours* (Columbia: University of South Carolina Press, 1994), p. 100.

4. Carl Sandburg, *Lincoln: The War Years* (Charles Scribner's Sons, New York: 1945), vol. 6, p. 260.

5. Elizabeth Keckley, *Behind the Scenes* (New York: G. W. Carlton & Co., 1868), pp. 137–138.

6. Reck, p. 16.

7. Gideon Welles, *Diary* (New York: W. W. Norton & Co., 1960), p. 526.

8. Jim Bishop, *The Day Lincoln Was Shot* (New York: Harper & Row, 1955), p. 158.

9. Carl Sandburg, *Abraham Lincoln* (New York: Harcourt Brace Jovanovich, Inc., 1974), p. 674.

10. Ibid., p. 703.

11. William Hayes Ward, *Tributes to Abraham Lincoln from His Associates* (New York: Thomas Y. Crowell & Co., 1895), p. 148.

12. Reck, p. 47.

13. William H. Crook, *Through Five Administrations* (New York: Harper Bros., 1910), p. 66.

14. Ibid., p. 67.

15. Bishop, p. 162.

16. Clara E. Laughlin, *The Death of Lincoln* (New York: Doubleday, Page & Co., 1909), p. 76.

Chapter 9

1. George J. Olszewski, *The Restoration of Ford's Theatre* (Washington, D.C.: National Park Service, 1963), p. 112.

2. John Deering, Jr., Letter to "My Dear Friend," April 26, 1865, Lincoln Museum, Fort Wayne, Ind.

3. W. Emerson Reck, *A. Lincoln: His Last 24 Hours* (Columbia: University of South Carolina Press, 1994), p. 102.

4. Jim Bishop, *The Day Lincoln Was Shot* (New York: Harper & Row, 1955), p. 208.

5. In David Colbert, ed., *Eyewitness to America: 500 Years of America in the Words of Those Who Saw It Happen* (New York: Pantheon Books, 1997), pp. 241–242.

6. Bishop, p. 209.

7. Ibid., p. 220.

8. Ibid., p. 222.

9. Ibid., p. 221.

10. Reck, p. 136.

Chapter 10

1. Charles Leale, "Lincoln's Last Hours," *Harper's Weekly,* February 13, 1909, p. 7.

2. O. H. Oldroyd, *The Assassination of Abraham Lincoln* (Washington, D.C.: O.H. Oldroyd, 1901), p. 107.

3. In David Colbert, ed., *Eyewitness to America: 500 Years of America in the Words of Those Who Saw It Happen* (New York: Pantheon Books, 1997), p. 245.

4. Leale, p. 27.

5. *The War of the Rebellion: Official Records*, U. S. War Department, vol. 46, no. 3, pp. 780–781.

6. Asia Booth Clarke, *The Unlocked Book* (New York: J.B. Putnam's Sons, 1938), p. 37.

7. Carl Sandburg, *Abraham Lincoln* (New York: Harcourt Brace Jovanovich, Inc., 1974), p. 725.

8. Ibid.

9. W. Emerson Reck, *A. Lincoln: His Last 24 Hours* (Columbia: University of South Carolina Press, 1994), p. 159.

Chapter 11

1. Carl Sandburg, *Abraham Lincoln* (New York: Harcourt Brace Jovanovich, Inc., 1974), p. 726.

2. Asia Booth Clarke, *The Unlocked Book* (New York: J.B. Putnam's Sons, 1938), p. 58.

3. Margaret Leech, *Reveille in Washington* (Alexandria, Va.: Time-Life Books, Inc., 1980), p. 504.

4. Ibid., p. 505.

5. Sandburg, p. 728.

6. Ibid., p. 726.

7. Ibid.

8. Ibid., p. 717.

9. Abraham Lincoln, *The Writings of Abraham Lincoln* (New York: Random House, 1940), p. 842.

★ FURTHER READING ★

Bishop, Jim. *The Day Lincoln Was Shot.* New York: Harper & Row, 1955.

Clarke, Asia Booth. *Unlocked Book: A Memoir of John Wilkes Booth by His Sister.* North Stratford, NH: Ayer Company Publishers, Inc., 1972.

Judson, Karen. *Abraham Lincoln.* Springfield, NJ: Enslow Publishers, Inc., 1998.

Leech, Margaret. *Reveille in Washington.* Alexandria, VA: Time-Life Books, Inc., 1980.

Reck, W. Emerson. *A. Lincoln: His Last 24 Hours.* Columbia: University of South Carolina Press, 1994.

Sandburg, Carl. *Abraham Lincoln.* New York: Harcourt Brace Jovanovich, Inc., 1974.

★ Index ★